THE
JESUS
PERSON
PROMISE
BOOK

Books by David Wilkerson

THE
JESUS
PERSON
PROMISE
BOOK

800 PROMISES FROM THE
WORD OF GOD

COMPILED BY

DAVID WILKERSON

Chosen

a division of Baker Publishing Group
Minneapolis, Minnesota

© 1972 by World Challenge, Inc.

Published by Chosen Books
11400 Hampshire Avenue South
Bloomington, Minnesota 55438
www.chosenbooks.com

Chosen Books is a division of
Baker Publishing Group, Grand Rapids, Michigan

ISBN 978-0-8007-9595-5 (yellow cover)
ISBN 978-0-8007-9594-8 (gift edition)

Previously published by Regal Books, also as *Promises to Live by . . . The Pocket Promise Book.*

This edition published 2015.

Printed in the United States of America

Cover design by Gearbox

15 16 17 18 19 20 21   7 6 5 4 3 2 1

When you gave your heart to Christ, you inherited a great wealth—
all the hundreds of promises God gave you in His Word.
These promises rightfully belong to you as a child of God.
You must claim them, believe them, and act upon them.

Because of his glory and excellence, he has given us great and precious promises. These are the promises that enable you to share his divine nature and escape the world's corruption caused by human desires.

2 Peter 1:4 NLT

Contents

God's Promises for Your Personal Needs

God's Promises for Your Future Needs

How to Make These Promises Work in Your Life

When you gave your heart to Christ and became a Jesus person, you inherited a great wealth—all the hundreds of promises God gave you in His Word.

These promises rightfully belong to you as a child of God. You must claim them, believe them, and act upon them. Here's how:

1. Take each promise to mean just exactly what it says. Don't try to interpret it, add to it, or read between the lines. Accept it literally.

2. Get your mind and heart in condition to believe the promises. God's Word says, "If I regard iniquity in my heart, the Lord will not hear me" (Psalm 66:18 NKJV). Be sure there is no sin in your life. If there is some sin (hatred, bitterness, jealousy, lust, for example), ask the Lord for His forgiveness. Pray to have your mind renewed in the Holy Ghost.

3. If there is a part of the promise that depends upon your action, you must be willing to do it—follow through. If it says "pray," then pray. If it next says "believe," then you must believe in order to expect God to act. God is ready to do His part. You must be ready also to do yours.

4. Now, after you have done these first three things, you must be willing to wait on the Lord's time in answering. The promised answer may come immediately. Then again—it may not. Just don't get uptight! God will keep His promise. If the answer is long in coming, you can remember that He has a perfect time and a perfect plan for your life. Meanwhile, you might read the promise section on "Patience."

Follow these four steps to claiming all the promises God has given you to use. Take time to read some of them in your Bible in the context of the whole chapter where it appears. If you find one verse especially helpful, memorize it. Then you'll have it at your fingertips. Always remember that whatever God said—He will do!

Carry this book with you at all times. Think of it as a Bible promise dictionary and refer to it for answers to all your questions and needs. Memorize all the key verses and use them daily to open God's storehouse of benefits. God cannot and will not break one of these promises. Every promise in this book is yours! Trust them. Stand on them. Believe them. Then you can say, "God said it. I believe it. That settles it."

*He was fully
convinced that
God is able to
do whatever he
promises.*

Romans 4:21 NLT

God's Promises
for Your Spiritual Needs

A. The blood of Jesus Christ cleanses you from sin.

1. The blood of Jesus his Son cleanses us from all sin.

1 John 1:7 ESV

2. In whom we have redemption through His blood, the forgiveness of sins.

Colossians 1:14 NKJV

3. He will save His people from their sins.

Matthew 1:21 NKJV

4. Jesus gave his life for our sins, just as God our Father planned, in order to rescue us from this evil world in which we live.

Galatians 1:4 NLT

5. If we confess our sins, He is faithful and just to forgive us our sins and to cleanse us from all unrighteousness.

1 John 1:9 NKJV

6. For this is my blood of the covenant, which is poured out for many for the forgiveness of sins.

Matthew 26:28 ESV

7. Behold, the Lamb of God, who takes away the sin of the world!

John 1:29 ESV

8. He was pierced for our rebellion, crushed for our sins. He was beaten so we could be whole. He was whipped so we could be healed.

Isaiah 53:5 NLT

9. Without the shedding of blood there is no forgiveness of sins.

Hebrews 9:22 TLB

10. In Him we have redemption through His blood, the forgiveness of sins, according to the riches of His grace.

Ephesians 1:7 NKJV

11. He himself bore our sins in his body on the tree, that we might die to sin and live to righteousness. By his wounds you have been healed.

1 Peter 2:24 ESV

12. With his own blood—not the blood of goats and calves—he entered the Most Holy Place once for all time and secured our redemption forever.

Hebrews 9:12 NLT

13. To him who loves us and has freed us from our sins by his blood.

Revelation 1:5 ESV

14. The blood of Christ, who through the eternal Spirit offered himself without blemish to God, purify our conscience from dead works to serve the living God.

Hebrews 9:14 ESV

15. But now in Christ Jesus you who once were far off have been brought near by the blood of Christ.

Ephesians 2:13 ESV

16. Knowing that you were ransomed from the futile ways inherited from your forefathers, not with perishable things such as silver or gold, but with the precious blood of Christ, like that of a lamb without blemish or spot.

1 Peter 1:18–19 ESV

17. And since by his blood he did all this for us as sinners, how much more will he do for us now that he has declared us not guilty? Now he will save us from all of God's wrath to come.

Romans 5:9 TLB

18. For Christ's death on the cross has made peace with God for all by his blood.

Colossians 1:20 TLB

19. When we were utterly helpless, Christ came at just the right time and died for us sinners.

Romans 5:6 NLT

20. But God showed his great love for us by sending Christ to die for us while we were still sinners.

Romans 5:8 TLB

B. Jesus Christ died to give you eternal life.

KEY VERSE

21. For God so loved the world, that he gave his only Son, that whoever believes in him should not perish but have eternal life.

John 3:16 ESV

22. Truly, truly, I say to you, whoever believes has eternal life.

John 6:47 ESV

23. For the wages of sin is death, but the gift of God is eternal life in Christ Jesus our Lord.

Romans 6:23 NKJV

24. I tell you the truth, those who listen to my message and believe in God who sent me have eternal life. They will never be condemned for their sins, but they have already passed from death into life.

John 5:24 NLT

25. This is the way to have eternal life—to know you, the only true God, and Jesus Christ, the one you sent to earth.

John 17:3 NLT

26. This is the promise that he made to us—eternal life.

1 John 2:25 ESV

27. This is the bread that came down from heaven, not like the bread the fathers ate, and died. Whoever feeds on this bread will live forever.

John 6:58 ESV

28. My sheep listen to my voice; I know them, and they follow me. I give them eternal life, and they will never perish. No one can snatch them away from me.

John 10:27–28 NLT

29. This is the testimony, that God gave us eternal life, and this life is in his Son.

1 John 5:11 ESV

30. I write these things to you who believe in the name of the Son of God that you may know that you have eternal life.

1 John 5:13 ESV

31. This truth gives them confidence that they have eternal life, which God—who does not lie—promised them before the world began.

Titus 1:2 NLT

32. God will redeem my soul from the power of the grave, for He shall receive me.

Psalm 49:15 NKJV

33. If the Spirit of him who raised Jesus from the dead dwells in you, he who raised Christ Jesus from the dead will also give life to your mortal bodies through his Spirit who dwells in you.

Romans 8:11 ESV

34. I am the resurrection and the life. Whoever believes in me, though he die, yet shall he live.

John 11:25 ESV

35. He who raised the Lord Jesus will raise us also with Jesus and bring us with you into his presence.

2 Corinthians 4:14 ESV

36. Since we believe that Jesus died and then came back to life again, we can also believe that when Jesus returns, God will bring back with him all the Christians who have died.

1 Thessalonians 4:14 TLB

37. And now he has made all of this plain to us by the coming of our Savior Jesus Christ, who broke the power of death and showed us the way of everlasting life through trusting him.

2 Timothy 1:10 TLB

38. We shall be saved by His life. . . . Those who receive the abundance of grace and of the gift of righteousness will reign in life through the one, Jesus Christ.

Romans 5:10, 17 NASB

39. The gift of God is eternal life in Christ Jesus our Lord.

Romans 6:23 NKJV

40. Christ came with this new agreement so that all who are invited may come and have forever all the wonders God has promised them. For Christ died to rescue them from the penalty of the sins they had committed while still under that old system.

Hebrews 9:15 TLB

41. For the one who sows to his own flesh will from the flesh reap corruption, but the one who sows to the Spirit will from the Spirit reap eternal life.

Galatians 6:8 ESV

42. Being justified by his grace we might become heirs according to the hope of eternal life.

Titus 3:7 ESV

43. O death, where is your victory? . . . O death, where is your sting? But thanks be to God, who gives us the victory through our Lord Jesus Christ.

1 Corinthians 15:55, 57 ESV

C. You can expect His presence in your life.

KEY VERSE

44. My presence will go with you, and I will give you rest.

Exodus 33:14 ESV

45. The upright shall dwell in your presence.

Psalm 140:13 ESV

46. The LORD is with you while you are with him. If you seek him, he will be found by you.

2 Chronicles 15:2 ESV

47. It is the LORD who goes before you. He will be with you; he will not leave you or forsake you. Do not fear or be dismayed.

Deuteronomy 31:8 ESV

48. Be sure of this—that I am with you always, even to the end of the world.

Matthew 28:20 TLB

49. I am the vine; you are the branches. Whoever abides in me and I in him, he it is that bears much fruit, for apart from me you can do nothing.

John 15:5 ESV

50. All who love me will do what I say. My Father will love them, and we will come and make our home with each of them.

John 14:23 NLT

51. I am the LORD your God and there is no other. My people shall never be put to shame.

Joel 2:27 NKJV

52. The LORD has set apart the godly for himself.

Psalm 4:3 ESV

53. The LORD loves the righteous.

Psalm 146:8 ESV

54. Look! I have been standing at the door and I am constantly knocking. If anyone hears me calling him and opens the door, I will come in and fellowship with him and he with me.

Revelation 3:20 TLB

55. For the LORD God is our sun and our shield. He gives us grace and glory. The LORD will withhold no good thing from those who do what is right.

Psalm 84:11 NLT

56. Salvation belongs to the LORD; your blessing be on your people!

Psalm 3:8 ESV

57. For all who are led by the Spirit of God are children of God.

Romans 8:14 NLT

D. You can expect answers to your prayers.

KEY VERSE

58. If you abide in me, and my words abide in you, ask whatever you wish, and it will be done for you.

John 15:7 ESV

59. Therefore I tell you, whatever you ask in prayer, believe that you have received it, and it will be yours.

Mark 11:24 ESV

60. You have given him his heart's desire and have not withheld the request of his lips.

Psalm 21:2 ESV

61. We know that all things work together for good to those who love God, to those who are the called according to His purpose.

Romans 8:28 NKJV

62. The LORD hears his people when they call to him for help. He rescues them from all their troubles.

Psalm 34:17 NLT

63. Be delighted with the Lord. Then he will give you all your heart's desires.

Psalm 37:4 TLB

64. Call upon me in the day of trouble; I will deliver you, and you shall glorify me.

Psalm 50:15 ESV

65. As for me, I will call upon God, and the LORD shall save me.

Psalm 55:16 NKJV

66. Morning, noon, and night I cry out in my distress, and the LORD hears my voice.

Psalm 55:17 NLT

67. In the day of my trouble I call upon you, for you answer me.

Psalm 86:7 esv

68. Ask, and it will be given to you; seek, and you will find; knock, and it will be opened to you.

Matthew 7:7 esv

69. It shall come to pass that before they call, I will answer; and while they are still speaking, I will hear.

Isaiah 65:24 nkjv

70. Call to me and I will answer you, and will tell you great and hidden things that you have not known.

Jeremiah 33:3 esv

71. Then you shall call, and the Lord will answer; you shall cry, and he will say, "Here I am."

Isaiah 58:9 esv

72. Yes, ask me for anything in my name, and I will do it!

John 14:14 nlt

73. When they call on me, I will answer; I will be with them in trouble. I will rescue and honor them.

Psalm 91:15 nlt

74. We will receive from him whatever we ask because we obey him and do the things that please him.

1 John 3:22 nlt

75. I also tell you this: If two of you agree here on earth concerning anything you ask, my Father in heaven will do it for you.

Matthew 18:19 nlt

76. If My people who are called by My name will humble themselves, and pray and seek My face, and turn from their wicked ways, then I will hear from heaven, and will forgive their sin and heal their land.

2 Chronicles 7:14 nkjv

77. Whatever you ask in prayer, you will receive, if you have faith.

Matthew 21:22 esv

78. For everyone who asks receives, and the one who seeks finds, and to the one who knocks it will be opened.

Luke 11:10 esv

79. This is the confidence that we have toward him, that if we ask anything according to his will he hears us.

1 John 5:14 ESV

80. If we know that he hears us in whatever we ask, we know that we have the requests that we have asked of him.

1 John 5:15 ESV

81. Since he did not spare even his own Son for us but gave him up for us all, won't he also surely give us everything else?

Romans 8:32 TLB

82. Commit your way to the LORD; trust in him, and he will act.

Psalm 37:5 ESV

83. Believe that there is a God and that he rewards those who sincerely look for him.

Hebrews 11:6 TLB

E. God will keep you.

KEY VERSE

84. Holy Father, keep through Your name those whom You have given Me.

John 17:11 NKJV

85. But the Lord is faithful. He will establish you and guard you against the evil one.

2 Thessalonians 3:3 ESV

86. My Father, who has given them to me, is greater than all, and no one is able to snatch them out of the Father's hand.

John 10:29 ESV

87. It is God who establishes us with you in Christ, and has anointed us.

2 Corinthians 1:21 ESV

88. . . . who will sustain you to the end, guiltless in the day of our Lord Jesus Christ.

1 Corinthians 1:8 ESV

89. I am certain that God, who began the good work within you, will continue his work until it is finally finished on the day when Christ Jesus returns.

Philippians 1:6 NLT

90. For I am persuaded that neither death nor life, nor angels nor principalities nor powers, nor things present nor things to come, nor height nor depth, nor any other created thing, shall be able to separate us from the love of God which is in Christ Jesus our Lord.

Romans 8:38–39 NKJV

91. But the righteous has an everlasting foundation.

Proverbs 10:25 NKJV

92. When I thought, "My foot slips," your steadfast love, O LORD, held me up.

Psalm 94:18 ESV

93. God is protecting you by his power until you receive this salvation.

1 Peter 1:5 NLT

94. Now all glory to God, who is able to keep you from falling away and will bring you with great joy into his glorious presence without a single fault.

Jude 24 NLT

95. Therefore, brothers, be all the more diligent to confirm your calling and election, for if you practice these qualities you will never fall.

2 Peter 1:10 ESV

96. No one who has become part of God's family makes a practice of sinning, for Christ, God's Son, holds him securely and the devil cannot get his hands on him.

1 John 5:18 TLB

97. God Himself will be with them and be their God.

Revelation 21:3 NKJV

98. You shall be my people and I will be your God.

Jeremiah 30:22 TLB

99. I will be their God, and they shall be My people.

2 Corinthians 6:16 NKJV

100. God is not ashamed to be called their God, for he has made a heavenly city for them.

Hebrews 11:16 TLB

101. He will feed his flock like a shepherd. He will carry the lambs in his arms, holding them close to his heart. He will gently lead the mother sheep with their young.

Isaiah 40:11 NLT

102. Though I walk in the midst of trouble, you preserve my life; you stretch out your hand against the wrath of my enemies, and your right hand delivers me.

Psalm 138:7 ESV

103. The LORD will be your confidence and will keep your foot from being caught.

Proverbs 3:26 ESV

104. The angel of the LORD encamps around those who fear him, and delivers them.

Psalm 34:7 ESV

105. I have set the LORD always before me; because He is at my right hand, I shall not be moved.

Psalm 16:8 NKJV

106. He is always watching, never sleeping. Jehovah himself is caring for you.

Psalm 121:4–5 TLB

107. For you are my hiding place; you protect me from trouble. You surround me with songs of victory.

Psalm 32:7 NLT

F. God will give you strength for His service.

KEY VERSE

108. Not by might, nor by power, but by my Spirit, says the LORD of hosts.

Zechariah 4:6 ESV

109. The God of Israel gives strength and mighty power to his people.

Psalm 68:35 TLB

110. But you will receive power when the Holy Spirit has come upon you, and you will be my witnesses in Jerusalem and in all Judea and Samaria, and to the end of the earth.

Acts 1:8 ESV

111. Trust in the LORD always, for the LORD God is the eternal Rock.

Isaiah 26:4 NLT

112. But to all who did receive him, who believed in his name, he gave the right to become children of God.

John 1:12 ESV

113. But those who wait on the LORD shall renew their strength; they shall mount up with wings like eagles, they shall run and not be weary, they shall walk and not faint.

Isaiah 40:31 NKJV

114. And He said to me, "My grace is sufficient for you, for My strength is made perfect in weakness."

2 Corinthians 12:9 NKJV

115. So use every piece of God's armor to resist the enemy whenever he attacks, and when it is all over, you will still be standing up.

Ephesians 6:13 TLB

116. Fear not, for I am with you; be not dismayed, for I am your God; I will strengthen you, I will help you, I will uphold you with my righteous right hand.

Isaiah 41:10 ESV

117. For God is working in you, giving you the desire and the power to do what pleases him.

Philippians 2:13 NLT

118. But the salvation of the righteous is from the LORD; He is their strength in the time of trouble.

Psalm 37:39 NKJV

119. I pray that from his glorious, unlimited resources he will empower you with inner strength through his Spirit.

Ephesians 3:16 NLT

120. I can do all things through him who strengthens me.

Philippians 4:13 ESV

121. We are praying, too, that you will be filled with his mighty, glorious strength so that you can keep going no matter what happens— always full of the joy of the Lord.

Colossians 1:11 TLB

122. The righteous shall move onward and forward; those with pure hearts shall become stronger and stronger.

Job 17:9 TLB

123. For we are his workmanship, created in Christ Jesus for good works, which God prepared beforehand, that we should walk in them.

Ephesians 2:10 ESV

124. I lift up my eyes to the hills. From where does my help come? My help comes from the LORD, who made heaven and earth.

Psalm 121:1–2 ESV

G. God will teach you truth.

KEY VERSE

125. I will instruct you (says the Lord) and guide you along the best pathway for your life; I will advise you and watch your progress.

Psalm 32:8 TLB

126. He knows just what to do, for God has made him see and understand.

Isaiah 28:26 TLB

127. For God, who said, "Let light shine out of darkness," has shone in our hearts to give the light of the knowledge of the glory of God in the face of Jesus Christ.

2 Corinthians 4:6 ESV

128. Come, let us go up to the mountain of the LORD, to the house of Jacob's God. There he will teach us his ways, and we will walk in his paths.

Isaiah 2:3 NLT

129. Who are those who fear the LORD? He will show them the path they should choose.

Psalm 25:12 NLT

130. Anyone who wants to do the will of God will know whether my teaching is from God or is merely my own.

John 7:17 NLT

131. He encircled him, he cared for him, he kept him as the apple of his eye.

Deuteronomy 32:10 ESV

132. I pray for you constantly, asking God, the glorious Father of our Lord Jesus Christ, to give you wisdom to see clearly and really understand who Christ is and all that he has done for you.

Ephesians 1:17 TLB

133. When the Spirit of truth comes, he will guide you into all the truth, for he will not speak on his own authority, but whatever he hears he will speak, and he will declare to you the things that are to come.

John 16:13 ESV

134. There are secrets the Lord your God has not revealed to us, but these words that he has revealed are for us and our children to obey forever.

Deuteronomy 29:29 TLB

135. All things that I heard from My Father I have made known to you.

John 15:15 NKJV

136. No mere man has ever seen, heard, or even imagined what wonderful things God has ready for those who love the Lord. But we know about these things because God has sent his Spirit to tell us, and his Spirit searches out and shows us all of God's deepest secrets.

1 Corinthians 2:9–10 TLB

137. He reveals profound mysteries beyond man's understanding. He knows all hidden things, for he is light, and darkness is no obstacle to him.

Daniel 2:22 TLB

138. Behold, the former things have come to pass, and new things I declare; before they spring forth I tell you of them.

Isaiah 42:9 NKJV

139. For now we see in a mirror dimly, but then face to face. Now I know in part; then I shall know fully, even as I have been fully known.

1 Corinthians 13:12 ESV

140. As it is written in the Scriptures, "They will all be taught by God." Everyone who listens to the Father and learns from him comes to me.

John 6:45 NLT

141. But the Helper, the Holy Spirit, whom the Father will send in my name, he will teach you all things and bring to your remembrance all that I have said to you.

John 14:26 ESV

142. From a wise mind comes careful and persuasive speech.

Proverbs 16:23 TLB

143. The humble He guides in justice, and the humble He teaches His way.

Psalm 25:9 NKJV

H. God will work miracles in your life.

> **KEY VERSE**
>
> **144.** "If you can!" All things are possible for one who believes.
>
> Mark 9:23 ESV

145. Truly, truly, I say to you, whoever believes in me will also do the works that I do; and greater works than these will he do, because I am going to the Father.

John 14:12 ESV

146. Whatever you ask in my name, this I will do, that the Father may be glorified in the Son.

John 14:13 ESV

147. Yes, ask me for anything in my name, and I will do it!

John 14:14 NLT

148. Now to him who is able to do far more abundantly than all that we ask or think, according to the power at work within us.

Ephesians 3:20 ESV

149. If you had faith even as small as a tiny mustard seed nothing would be impossible.

Matthew 17:20 TLB

150. If two of you agree here on earth concerning anything you ask, my Father in heaven will do it for you.

Matthew 18:19 NLT

151. And God has appointed in the church first apostles, second prophets, third teachers, then miracles, then gifts of healing, helping, administrating, and various kinds of tongues.

1 Corinthians 12:28 ESV

152. He gives one person the power to perform miracles, and another the ability to prophesy. He gives someone else the ability to discern whether a message is from the Spirit of God or from another spirit. Still another person is given the ability to speak in unknown languages, while another is given the ability to interpret what is being said.

1 Corinthians 12:10 NLT

I. God will fill your life with love.

KEY VERSE

153. So we have come to know and to believe the love that God has for us. God is love, and whoever abides in love abides in God, and God abides in him.

1 John 4:16 ESV

154. If you keep my commandments, you will abide in my love, just as I have kept my Father's commandments and abide in his love.

John 15:10 ESV

155. Hatred stirs old quarrels, but love overlooks insults.

Proverbs 10:12 TLB

156. The LORD preserves all who love him, but all the wicked he will destroy.

Psalm 145:20 ESV

157. Those who accept my commandments and obey them are the ones who love me. And because they love me, my Father will love them. And I will love them and reveal myself to each of them.

John 14:21 NLT

158. The person who truly loves God is the one who is open to God's knowledge.

1 Corinthians 8:3 TLB

159. As the Father has loved me, so have I loved you. Abide in my love.

John 15:9 ESV

160. I know it is important to love him with all my heart and all my understanding and all my strength, and to love my neighbor as myself. This is more important than to offer all of the burnt offerings and sacrifices required in the law.

Mark 12:33 NLT

161. No eye has seen, nor ear heard, nor the heart of man imagined, what God has prepared for those who love him.

1 Corinthians 2:9 ESV

162. . . . to know the love of Christ that surpasses knowledge, that you may be filled with all the fullness of God.

Ephesians 3:19 ESV

163. This is real love—not that we loved God, but that he loved us and sent his Son as a sacrifice to take away our sins.

1 John 4:10 NLT

164. Beloved, let us love one another, for love is from God, and whoever loves has been born of God and knows God.

1 John 4:7 ESV

165. Nor height nor depth, nor anything else in all creation, will be able to separate us from the love of God in Christ Jesus our Lord.

Romans 8:39 ESV

166. Though we have never yet seen God, when we love each other God lives in us and his love within us grows ever stronger.

1 John 4:12 TLB

167. We need have no fear of someone who loves us perfectly; his perfect love for us eliminates all dread of what he might do to us. If we are afraid, it is for fear of what he might do to us, and shows that we are not fully convinced that he really loves us.

1 John 4:18 TLB

168. I love those who love me, and those who seek me diligently will find me.

Proverbs 8:17 NKJV

169. There are three things that remain—faith, hope, and love—and the greatest of these is love.

1 Corinthians 13:13 TLB

J. You can grow spiritually.

KEY VERSE

170. And we all, with unveiled face, beholding the glory of the Lord, are being transformed into the same image from one degree of glory to another. For this comes from the Lord who is the Spirit.

2 Corinthians 3:18 ESV

171. That Christ will be more and more at home in your hearts, living within you as you trust in him. May your roots go down deep into the soil of God's marvelous love; and may you be able to feel and understand, as all God's children should, how long, how wide, how deep, and how high his love really is; and to experience this love for yourselves, though it is so great that you will never see the end of it or fully know or understand it. And so at last you will be filled up with God himself.

Ephesians 3:17–19 TLB

172. The godly will flourish like palm trees and grow strong like the cedars of Lebanon.

Psalm 92:12 NKJV

173. Like newborn infants, long for the pure spiritual milk, that by it you may grow up into salvation—if indeed you have tasted that the Lord is good.

1 Peter 2:2–3 ESV

174. But the path of the righteous is like the light of dawn, which shines brighter and brighter until full day.

Proverbs 4:18 ESV

175. He humbled you by letting you go hungry and then feeding you with manna, a food previously unknown to you and your ancestors. He did it to teach you that people do not live by bread alone; rather, we live by every word that comes from the mouth of the LORD.

Deuteronomy 8:3 NLT

176. And I am sure of this, that he who began a good work in you will bring it to completion at the day of Jesus Christ.

Philippians 1:6 ESV

177. Then we will no longer be immature like children. We won't be tossed and blown about by every wind of new teaching. We will not be influenced when people try to trick us with lies so clever they sound like the truth. Instead, we will speak the truth in love, growing in every way more and more like Christ, who is the head of his body, the church.

Ephesians 4:14–15 NLT

178. So as to walk in a manner worthy of the Lord, fully pleasing to him, bearing fruit in every good work and increasing in the knowledge of God.

Colossians 1:10 ESV

179. My prayer for you is that you will overflow more and more with love for others, and at the same time keep on growing in spiritual knowledge and insight, for I want you always to see clearly the difference between right and wrong, and to be inwardly clean, no one being able to criticize you from now until our Lord returns.

Philippians 1:9–10 TLB

180. For this very reason, make every effort to supplement your faith with virtue, and virtue with knowledge, and knowledge with self-control, and self-control with steadfastness, and steadfastness with godliness, and godliness with brotherly affection, and brotherly affection with love. For if these qualities are yours and are increasing, they keep you from being ineffective or unfruitful in the knowledge of our Lord Jesus Christ.

2 Peter 1:5–8 ESV

K. The Lord will baptize you in the Holy Spirit.

181. I baptize you with water for repentance, but he who is coming after me is mightier than I, whose sandals I am not worthy to carry. He will baptize you with the Holy Spirit and fire.

Matthew 3:11 ESV

182. Blessed are those who hunger and thirst for righteousness, for they shall be filled.

Matthew 5:6 NKJV

183. I will put my Spirit within you so that you will obey my laws and do whatever I command.

Ezekiel 36:27 TLB

184. I will ask the Father and he will give you another Comforter, and he will never leave you. He is the Holy Spirit, the Spirit who leads into all truth. The world at large cannot receive him, for it isn't looking for him and doesn't recognize him. But you do, for he lives with you now and some day shall be in you.

John 14:16–17 TLB

185. Do you not know that you are God's temple and that God's Spirit dwells in you?

1 Corinthians 3:16 ESV

186. But you will receive power when the Holy Spirit has come upon you, and you will be my witnesses in Jerusalem and in all Judea and Samaria, and to the end of the earth.

Acts 1:8 ESV

187. Each one of you must turn from sin, return to God, and be baptized in the name of Jesus Christ for the forgiveness of your sins; then you also shall receive this gift, the Holy Spirit.

Acts 2:38 TLB

188. If even sinful persons like yourselves give children what they need, don't you realize that your heavenly Father will do at least as much, and give the Holy Spirit to those who ask for him?

Luke 11:13 TLB

189. This promise is to you, to your children, and to those far away—all who have been called by the Lord our God.

Acts 2:39 NLT

190. It shall come to pass afterward that I will pour out My Spirit on all flesh; your sons and your daughters shall prophesy, your old men shall dream dreams, your young men shall see visions.

Joel 2:28 NKJV

191. But the Helper, the Holy Spirit, whom the Father will send in my name, he will teach you all things and bring to your remembrance all that I have said to you.

John 14:26 ESV

192. For by one Spirit are we all baptized into one body.

1 Corinthians 12:13 NKJV

193. I will send you the Comforter—the Holy Spirit, the source of all truth. He will come to you from the Father and will tell you all about me.

John 15:26 TLB

194. Nevertheless I tell you the truth. It is to your advantage that I go away; for if I do not go away, the Helper will not come to you; but if I depart, I will send Him to you.

John 16:7 NKJV

195. Now we have received, not the spirit of the world, but the Spirit who is from God, that we might know the things that have been freely given to us by God.

1 Corinthians 2:12 NKJV

196. Through Christ Jesus, God has blessed the Gentiles with the same blessing he promised to Abraham, so that we who are believers might receive the promised Holy Spirit through faith.

Galatians 3:14 NLT

197. Whoever drinks of the water that I will give him will never be thirsty again. The water that I will give him will become in him a spring of water welling up to eternal life.

John 4:14 ESV

198. Surely I will pour out my spirit on you; I will make my words known to you.

Proverbs 1:23 NKJV

199. He has put his brand upon us—his mark of ownership—and given us his Holy Spirit in our hearts as guarantee that we belong to him, and as the first installment of all that he is going to give us.

2 Corinthians 1:22 TLB

200. In him you also, when you heard the word of truth, the gospel of your salvation, and believed in him, were sealed with the promised Holy Spirit.

Ephesians 1:13 ESV

L. God will give you a new freedom.

KEY VERSE

201. If the Son sets you free, you are truly free.

John 8:36 NLT

202. You will know the truth, and the truth will set you free.

John 8:32 TLB

203. When the Spirit of truth comes, he will guide you into all truth.

John 16:13 NLT

204. Because you belong to him, the power of the life-giving Spirit has freed you from the power of sin that leads to death.

Romans 8:2 NLT

205. For the Lord is the Spirit, and wherever the Spirit of the Lord is, there is freedom.

2 Corinthians 3:17 NLT

206. Thou shalt break the yoke of their burden and the staff on their shoulders, the rod of their oppressor.

Isaiah 9:4 NASB

207. Now you are free from the power of sin and are slaves of God, and his benefits to you include holiness and everlasting life.

Romans 6:22 TLB

208. The LORD keeps you from all harm and watches over your life. The LORD keeps watch over you as you come and go, both now and forever.

Psalm 121:7–8 NLT

209. He has sent me to comfort the brokenhearted and to proclaim that captives will be released and prisoners will be freed.

Isaiah 61:1 NLT

M. God instills faith in you.

KEY VERSE

210. God has dealt to each one a measure of faith.

Romans 12:3 NKJV

211. For by grace you have been saved through faith, and that not of yourselves; it is the gift of God.

Ephesians 2:8 NKJV

212. But the Holy Spirit produces this kind of fruit in our lives: love, joy, peace, patience, kindness, goodness, faithfulness, gentleness, and self-control.

Galatians 5:22–23 NLT

213. Though you have not seen him, you love him. Though you do not now see him, you believe in him and rejoice with joy that is inexpressible and filled with glory, obtaining the outcome of your faith, the salvation of your souls.

1 Peter 1:8–9 ESV

214. Now the just shall live by faith.

Hebrews 10:38 NKJV

215. You can never please God without faith, without depending on him. Anyone who wants to come to God must believe that there is a God and that he rewards those who sincerely look for him.

Hebrews 11:6 TLB

216. For you know that the testing of your faith produces stead-fastness.

James 1:3 ESV

217. These trials will show that your faith is genuine. It is being tested as fire tests and purifies gold—though your faith is far more precious than mere gold. So when your faith remains strong through many trials, it will bring you much praise and glory and honor on the day when Jesus Christ is revealed to the whole world.

1 Peter 1:7 NLT

218. The man who finds life will find it through trusting God.

Romans 1:17 TLB

219. But the Scripture imprisoned everything under sin, so that the promise by faith in Jesus Christ might be given to those who believe.

Galatians 3:22 ESV

220. For now we are all children of God through faith in Jesus Christ.

Galatians 3:26 TLB

221. For you have been given not only the privilege of trusting in Christ but also the privilege of suffering for him.

Philippians 1:29 NLT

222. For everyone who has been born of God overcomes the world. And this is the victory that has overcome the world—our faith.

1 John 5:4 ESV

223. So faith comes from hearing, and hearing through the word of Christ.

Romans 10:17 ESV

224. Be not slothful, but followers of them who through faith and patience inherit the promises.

Hebrews 6:12 KJV

225. Anything is possible if you have faith.

Mark 9:23 TLB

226. Believe in the LORD your God, and you will be able to stand firm. Believe in his prophets, and you will succeed.

2 Chronicles 20:20 NLT

227. In every battle you will need faith as your shield to stop the fiery arrows aimed at you by Satan.

Ephesians 6:16 TLB

228. Believe in the Lord Jesus and you will be saved, along with everyone in your household.

Acts 16:31 NLT

229. Blessed are those who have not seen and yet have believed.

John 20:29 NKJV

230. For truly, I say to you, if you have faith like a grain of mustard seed, you will say to this mountain, "Move from here to there," and it will move, and nothing will be impossible for you.

Matthew 17:20 ESV

231. Truly if you have faith, and don't doubt, you can do things like this and much more. You can even say to this Mount of Olives "move over into the ocean," and it will.

Matthew 21:21 TLB

232. Truly, I say to you, whoever says to this mountain, "Be taken up and thrown into the sea," and does not doubt in his heart, but believes that what he says will come to pass, it will be done for him.

Mark 11:23 ESV

233. You can get anything—anything you ask for in prayer—if you believe.

Matthew 21:22 TLB

234. But if you stay in me and obey my commands, you may ask any request you like, and it will be granted!

John 15:7 TLB

235. Until now you have asked nothing in My name. Ask, and you will receive, that your joy may be full.

John 16:24 NKJV

236. We will receive from him whatever we ask because we obey him and do the things that please him.

1 John 3:22 NLT

237. And this is the confidence that we have toward him, that if we ask anything according to his will he hears us. And if we know that he hears us in whatever we ask, we know that we have the requests that we have asked of him.

1 John 5:14–15 ESV

238. Fight the good fight for the true faith. Hold tightly to the eternal life to which God has called you, which you have declared so well before many witnesses.

1 Timothy 6:12 NLT

239. You can ask for anything in my name, and I will do it, so that the Son can bring glory to the Father.

John 14:13 NLT

240. Yes, ask me for anything in my name, and I will do it!

John 14:14 NLT

241. So now, since we have been made right in God's sight by faith in his promises, we can have real peace with him because of what Jesus Christ our Lord has done for us.

Romans 5:1 TLB

N, Jesus Christ forgives your sins daily.

KEY VERSE

242. If anyone sins, we have an Advocate with the Father, Jesus Christ the righteous.

1 John 2:1 NKJV

243. Your sins have been forgiven in the name of Jesus our Savior.

1 John 2:12 TLB

244. If we confess our sins, He is faithful and just to forgive us our sins and to cleanse us from all unrighteousness.

1 John 1:9 NKJV

245. Sanctify them in the truth; your word is truth.

John 17:17 ESV

246. Now may the God of peace make you holy in every way, and may your whole spirit and soul and body be kept blameless until our Lord Jesus Christ comes again.

1 Thessalonians 5:23 NLT

247. And you, who once were alienated and hostile in mind, doing evil deeds, he has now reconciled in his body of flesh by his death, in order to present you holy and blameless and above reproach before him.

Colossians 1:21–22 ESV

248. Your sins are washed away, and you are set apart for God, and he has accepted you because of what the Lord Jesus Christ and the Spirit of our God have done for you.

1 Corinthians 6:11 TLB

249. He gave his life to free us from every kind of sin, to cleanse us, and to make us his very own people, totally committed to doing good deeds.

Titus 2:14 NLT

250. I will turn my hand against you and will smelt away your dross as with lye and remove all your alloy.

Isaiah 1:25 ESV

251. To him all the prophets bear witness that everyone who believes in him receives forgiveness of sins through his name.

Acts 10:43 ESV

252. For God took the sinless Christ and poured into him our sins. Then, in exchange, he poured God's goodness into us.

2 Corinthians 5:21 TLB

253. By him everyone who believes is freed from everything from which you could not be freed by the law of Moses.

Acts 13:39 ESV

254. He does not punish us for all our sins; he does not deal harshly with us, as we deserve. For his unfailing love toward those who fear him is as great as the height of the heavens above the earth.

Psalm 103:10–11 NLT

O. The Lord brings hope to you.

255. O Lord, you alone are my hope; I've trusted you from childhood.

Psalm 71:5 TLB

256. The LORD will redeem those who serve him. No one who takes refuge in him will be condemned.

Psalm 34:22 NLT

257. You will have courage because you will have hope.

Job 11:18 TLB

258. The LORD watches over those who fear him, those who rely on his unfailing love. He rescues them from death and keeps them alive in times of famine.

Psalm 33:18–19 NLT

259. Everyone who thus hopes in him purifies himself as he is pure.

1 John 3:3 ESV

260. The LORD shall help them and deliver them; He shall deliver them from the wicked, and save them, because they trust in Him.

Psalm 37:40 NKJV

261. For God wanted them to know that the riches and glory of Christ are for you Gentiles, too. And this is the secret: Christ lives in you. This gives you assurance of sharing his glory.

Colossians 1:27 NLT

262. O my soul, don't be discouraged. Don't be upset. Expect God to act! For I know that I shall again have plenty of reason to praise him for all that he will do. He is my help! He is my God!

Psalm 42:11 TLB

263. We who have fled for refuge might have strong encouragement to hold fast to the hope set before us. We have this as a sure and steadfast anchor of the soul, a hope that enters into the inner place behind the curtain.

Hebrews 6:18–19 ESV

264. Be strong, and let your heart take courage, all you who wait for the Lord!

Psalm 31:24 ESV

265. I am not ashamed, for I know whom I have believed and am persuaded that He is able to keep what I have committed to Him until that Day.

2 Timothy 1:12 NKJV

266. For this great God is our God forever and ever. He will be our guide until we die.

Psalm 48:14 TLB

267. And hope does not put us to shame, because God's love has been poured into our hearts through the Holy Spirit who has been given to us.

Romans 5:5 ESV

268. For whatever was written in former days was written for our instruction, that through endurance and through the encouragement of the Scriptures we might have hope.

Romans 15:4 ESV

269. We confidently and joyfully look forward to sharing God's glory.

Romans 5:2 NLT

P. The Word of God is alive.

KEY VERSE

270. Heaven and earth shall pass away, but my words shall not pass away.

Matthew 24:35 KJV

271. The grass withers, the flowers fade, but the word of our God shall stand forever.

Isaiah 40:8 TLB

272. The word of the Lord will last forever. And his message is the Good News that was preached to you.

1 Peter 1:25 TLB

273. All Scripture is inspired by God and is useful to teach us what is true and to make us realize what is wrong in our lives. It corrects us when we are wrong and teaches us to do what is right.

2 Timothy 3:16 NLT

274. Thy word is a lamp unto my feet, and a light unto my path.

Psalm 119:105 KJV

275. I am not ashamed of the gospel of Christ, for it is the power of God to salvation for everyone who believes.

Romans 1:16 NKJV

276. For the word of God is living and powerful, and sharper than any two-edged sword, piercing even to the division of soul and spirit, and of joints and marrow, and is a discerner of the thoughts and intents of the heart.

Hebrews 4:12 NKJV

277. Take the helmet of salvation, and the sword of the Spirit, which is the word of God.

Ephesians 6:17 NKJV

278. Man does not live by bread alone, but man lives by every word that comes from the mouth of the LORD.

Deuteronomy 8:3 ESV

279. Like newborn infants, long for the pure spiritual milk, that by it you may grow up into salvation—if indeed you have tasted that the Lord is good.

1 Peter 2:2–3 ESV

280. Work hard so you can present yourself to God and receive his approval. Be a good worker, one who does not need to be ashamed and who correctly explains the word of truth.

2 Timothy 2:15 NLT

281. You search the Scriptures, for you believe they give you eternal life. And the Scriptures point to me!

John 5:39 TLB

282. The law of the LORD is perfect, converting the soul; The testimony of the LORD is sure, making wise the simple; The statutes of the

LORD are right, rejoicing the heart; The commandment of the LORD is pure, enlightening the eye.

Psalm 19:7–8 NKJV

283. The sacred writings, which are able to make you wise for salvation through faith in Christ Jesus.

2 Timothy 3:15 ESV

284. The commandment is a lamp; and the law is a light; Reproofs of instruction are the way of life.

Proverbs 6:23 NKJV

285. Those who love your instructions have great peace and do not stumble.

Psalm 119:165 NLT

286. All who fear God and trust in him are blessed beyond expression. Yes, happy is the man who delights in doing his commands.

Psalm 112:1 TLB

287. So shall my word be that goes out from my mouth; it shall not return to me empty, but it shall accomplish that which I purpose, and shall succeed in the thing for which I sent it.

Isaiah 55:11 ESV

288. So faith comes from hearing, and hearing through the word of Christ.

Romans 10:17 ESV

289. Blessed is the one who reads aloud the words of this prophecy, and blessed are those who hear, and who keep what is written in it, for the time is near.

Revelation 1:3 ESV

Q. God honors obedience.

KEY VERSE

290. Keep putting into practice all you learned from me and saw me doing, and the God of peace will be with you.

Philippians 4:9 TLB

291. Blessed are they who observe justice, who do righteousness at all times!

Psalm 106:3 ESV

292. Has the Lord as much pleasure in your burnt offerings and sacrifices as in your obedience? Obedience is far better than sacrifice.

1 Samuel 15:22 TLB

293. If you will obey me and keep your part of my contract with you, you shall be my own little flock from among all the nations of the earth; for all the earth is mine.

Exodus 19:5 TLB

294. If you keep my commandments, you will abide in my love, just as I have kept my Father's commandments and abide in his love.

John 15:10 ESV

295. Anyone who listens to my teaching and follows it is wise, like a person who builds a house on solid rock.

Matthew 7:24 NLT

296. Jesus replied, "All who love me will do what I say. My Father will love them, and we will come and make our home with each of them.

John 14:23 NLT

297. If anyone breaks the least commandment, and teaches others to, he shall be the least in the Kingdom of Heaven. But those who teach God's laws and obey them shall be great in the Kingdom of Heaven.

Matthew 5:19 TLB

298. If anyone serves me, he must follow me; and where I am, there will my servant be also. If anyone serves me, the Father will honor him.

John 12:26 ESV

299. Not everyone who calls out to me, "Lord! Lord!" will enter the Kingdom of Heaven. Only those who actually do the will of my Father in heaven will enter.

Matthew 7:21 NLT

300. Whoever keeps doing the will of God will live forever.

1 John 2:17 TLB

301. I have given you an example to follow: do as I have done to you. . . . You know these things—now do them! That is the path of blessing.

John 13:15, 17 TLB

302. Anyone who wants to do the will of God will know whether my teaching is from God or is merely my own.

John 7:17 NLT

303. We will receive from him whatever we ask because we obey him and do the things that please him.

1 John 3:22 NLT

304. Obey the laws of God and follow all his ways; keep each of his commands written in the law of Moses so that you will prosper in everything you do, wherever you turn.

1 Kings 2:3 TLB

305. The LORD leads with unfailing love and faithfulness all who keep his covenant and obey his demands.

Psalm 25:10 NLT

306. If you are willing and obedient, you shall eat the good of the land.

Isaiah 1:19 ESV

307. But what I told them was: Obey me and I will be your God and you shall be my people; only do as I say and all shall be well.

Jeremiah 7:23 TLB

308. And now, O sons, listen to me: blessed are those who keep my ways.

Proverbs 8:32 ESV

309. Return to me, and I will return to you, says the LORD of hosts.

Malachi 3:7 ESV

310. If they listen and obey God, they will be blessed with prosperity throughout their lives. All their years will be pleasant.

Job 36:11 NKJV

311. Joyful are those who obey his laws and search for him with all their hearts.

Psalm 119:2 NLT

312. Keep the commandments and keep your life; despising them means death.

Proverbs 19:16 TLB

313. But the one who looks into the perfect law, the law of liberty, and perseveres, being no hearer who forgets but a doer who acts, he will be blessed in his doing.

James 1:25 ESV

314. He became the author of eternal salvation to all who obey Him.

Hebrews 5:9 NKJV

315. Blessed are those who do His commandments, that they may have the right to the tree of life, and may enter through the gates into the city.

Revelation 22:14 NKJV

R. God leaves surrender up to you.

KEY VERSE

316. Blessed are the poor in spirit, for theirs is the kingdom of heaven.

Matthew 5:3 NKJV

317. Take my yoke upon you, and learn from me, for I am gentle and lowly in heart, and you will find rest for your souls.

Matthew 11:29 ESV

318. If you will humble yourselves under the mighty hand of God, in his good time he will lift you up.

1 Peter 5:6 TLB

319. Blessed are all who hear the word of God and put it into practice.

Luke 11:28 NLT

320. Be subject for the Lord's sake to every human institution, whether it be to the emperor as supreme, or to governors as sent by him to punish those who do evil and to praise those who do good.

1 Peter 2:13–14 ESV

321. Likewise, you who are younger, be subject to the elders. Clothe yourselves, all of you, with humility toward one another, for "God opposes the proud but gives grace to the humble."

1 Peter 5:5 ESV

322. Whoever humbles himself as this little child is the greatest in the kingdom of heaven.

Matthew 18:4 NKJV

323. Submit to God. Resist the devil and he will flee from you.

James 4:7 NKJV

324. Humble yourselves before the Lord, and he will exalt you.

James 4:10 ESV

325. It is good both to hope and wait quietly for the salvation of the Lord.

Lamentations 3:26 TLB

326. True humility and respect for the Lord lead a man to riches, honor, and long life.

Proverbs 22:4 TLB

327. Jesus replied, "I am the Bread of Life. No one coming to me will ever be hungry again."

John 6:35 TLB

328. All that the Father gives me will come to me, and whoever comes to me I will never cast out.

John 6:37 ESV

S. God honors holiness.

KEY VERSE

329. Godliness is profitable for all things, having promise of the life that now is and of that which is to come.

1 Timothy 4:8 NKJV

330. Don't copy the behavior and customs of this world, but let God transform you into a new person by changing the way you think. Then you will learn to know God's will for you, which is good and pleasing and perfect.

Romans 12:2 NLT

331. Be anxious for nothing, but in everything by prayer and supplication, with thanksgiving, let your requests be made known to God; and the peace of God, which surpasses all understanding, will guard your hearts and minds through Christ Jesus.

Philippians 4:6–7 NKJV

332. Draw near to God, and he will draw near to you. Cleanse your hands, you sinners, and purify your hearts, you double-minded.

James 4:8 ESV

333. Righteousness will go before Him, and shall make His footsteps our pathway.

Psalm 85:13 NKJV

334. Whoever pursues righteousness and unfailing love will find life, righteousness, and honor.

Proverbs 21:21 NLT

335. Yet the Lord pleads with you still: Ask where the good road is, the godly paths you used to walk in, in the days of long ago. Travel there, and you will find rest for your souls.

Jeremiah 6:16 TLB

336. One who sows righteousness gets a sure reward.

Proverbs 11:18 ESV

337. For you bless the godly, O LORD; you surround them with your shield of love.

Psalm 5:12 NLT

338. And a highway shall be there, and it shall be called the Way of Holiness.

Isaiah 35:8 ESV

339. I have come as a Light to shine in this dark world, so that all who put their trust in me will no longer wander in the darkness.

John 12:46 TLB

340. O LORD, who shall sojourn in your tent? Who shall dwell on your holy hill? He who walks blamelessly and does what is right and speaks truth in his heart.

Psalm 15:1–2 ESV

341. For the LORD is righteous; he loves righteous deeds; the upright shall behold his face.

Psalm 11:7 ESV

342. For the eyes of the LORD move to and fro throughout the earth that he may strongly support those whose heart is completely his.

2 Chronicles 16:9 NASB

343. If our consciences are clear, we can come to the Lord with perfect assurance and trust.

1 John 3:21 TLB

344. The Lord observes the good deeds done by godly men, and gives them eternal rewards.

Psalm 37:18 TLB

345. For to set the mind on the flesh is death, but to set the mind on the Spirit is life and peace.

Romans 8:6 ESV

346. Joyful are people of integrity, who follow the instructions of the LORD.

Psalm 119:1 NLT

347. But the blameless in their ways are His delight.

Proverbs 11:20 NKJV

348. He stores up sound wisdom for the upright; he is a shield to those who walk in integrity.

Proverbs 2:7 ESV

349. I will honor those who honor me.

1 Samuel 2:30 NLT

T. God blesses clean conversation.

KEY VERSE

350. Those who walk my paths will receive salvation from the Lord.

Psalm 50:23 TLB

351. Do you want a long, good life? Then watch your tongue! Keep your lips from lying.

Psalm 34:12–13 TLB

352. Gentle words are a tree of life.

Proverbs 15:4 NLT

353. Everyone enjoys giving good advice, and how wonderful it is to be able to say the right thing at the right time.

Proverbs 15:23 TLB

354. The words you say will either acquit you or condemn you.

Matthew 12:37 NLT

355. If you confess with your mouth that Jesus is Lord and believe in your heart that God raised him from the dead, you will be saved. For with the heart one believes and is justified, and with the mouth one confesses and is saved.

Romans 10:9–10 ESV

356. Kind words are like honey—sweet to the soul and healthy for the body.

Proverbs 16:24 NLT

357. Whoever keeps his mouth and his tongue keeps himself out of trouble.

Proverbs 21:23 ESV

358. He who has clean hands and a pure heart, who does not lift up his soul to what is false and does not swear deceitfully. He will receive blessing from the LORD and righteousness from the God of his salvation.

Psalm 24:4–5 ESV

359. Whoever confesses that Jesus is the Son of God, God abides in him, and he in God.

1 John 4:15 ESV

360. So everyone who acknowledges me before men, I also will acknowledge before my Father who is in heaven.

Matthew 10:32 ESV

361. From a wise mind comes careful and persuasive speech.

Proverbs 16:23 TLB

362. The mouth of the righteous brings forth wisdom.

Proverbs 10:31 ESV

363. The lips of the righteous know what is acceptable.

Proverbs 10:32 NKJV

364. For I will give you the right words and such logic that none of your opponents will be able to reply!

Luke 21:15 TLB

365. To one is given the word of wisdom through the Spirit, to another the word of knowledge through the same Spirit.

1 Corinthians 12:8 NKJV

366. The preparations of the heart belong to man, but the answer of the tongue is from the LORD.

Proverbs 16:1 NKJV

367. Keep your life free from love of money, and be content with what you have, for he has said, "I will never leave you nor forsake you."

Hebrews 13:5 ESV

368. He who would love life and see good days, let him refrain his tongue from evil, and his lips from speaking deceit.

1 Peter 3:10 NKJV

369. Truth stands the test of time; lies are soon exposed.

Proverbs 12:19 TLB

370. O LORD, who shall sojourn in your tent? Who shall dwell on your holy hill? He who walks blamelessly and does what is right and speaks truth in his heart; who does not slander with his tongue and does no evil to his neighbor, nor takes up a reproach against his friend.

Psalm 15:1–3 ESV

371. A gentle answer turns away wrath, but harsh words cause quarrels.

Proverbs 15:1 TLB

U. God will bless your family.

KEY VERSE

372. I will give them one heart and one purpose: to worship me forever, for their own good and for the good of all their descendants.

Jeremiah 32:39 NLT

373. May the Lord richly bless both you and your children.

Psalm 115:14 TLB

374. You must obey these laws that I will tell you today, so that all will be well with you and your children.

Deuteronomy 4:40 TLB

375. The righteous who walks in his integrity—blessed are his children after him!

Proverbs 20:7 ESV

376. Those who fear the LORD are secure; he will be a refuge for their children.

Proverbs 14:26 NLT

377. You shall rejoice in all the good that the LORD your God has given to you and to your house.

Deuteronomy 26:11 ESV

378. Children are a gift from God.

Psalm 127:3 TLB

379. The father of the righteous will greatly rejoice; he who fathers a wise son will be glad in him.

Proverbs 23:24 ESV

380. Children, obey your parents in all things, for this is well pleasing to the Lord.

Colossians 3:20 TLB

381. Honor your father and mother. This is the first of God's Ten Commandments that ends with a promise. And this is the promise: that if you honor your father and mother, yours will be a long life, full of blessing.

Ephesians 6:2–3 TLB

382. Train up a child in the way he should go, and when he is old he will not depart from it.

Proverbs 22:6 NKJV

V. God prospers the charitable.

383. When you did it to one of the least of these my brothers and sisters, you were doing it to me!

Matthew 25:40 NLT

384. For truly, I say to you, whoever gives you a cup of water to drink because you belong to Christ will by no means lose his reward.

Mark 9:41 ESV

385. If you give to the poor, your needs will be supplied!

Proverbs 28:27 TLB

386. If you pour yourself out for the hungry and satisfy the desire of the afflicted, then shall your light rise in the darkness and your gloom be as the noonday.

Isaiah 58:10 ESV

387. Bring all the tithes into the storehouse so that there will be food enough in my Temple; if you do, I will open up the windows of heaven for you and pour out a blessing so great you won't have room enough to take it in!

Malachi 3:10 TLB

388. Whoever brings blessing will be enriched, and one who waters will himself be watered.

Proverbs 11:25 ESV

389. If you give little, you will get little. A farmer who plants just a few seeds will get only a small crop, but if he plants much, he will reap much.

2 Corinthians 9:6 TLB

390. Blessed are the merciful, for they shall obtain mercy.

Matthew 5:7 NKJV

391. Everyone must make up his own mind as to how much he should give. Don't force anyone to give more than he really wants to, for cheerful givers are the ones God prizes.

2 Corinthians 9:7 TLB

392. Take courage! Do not let your hands be weak, for your work shall be rewarded.

2 Chronicles 15:7 ESV

393. God blesses those who are kind to the poor. He helps them out of their troubles.

Psalm 41:1 TLB

394. God is able to make all grace abound to you, so that having all sufficiency in all things at all times, you may abound in every good work.

2 Corinthians 9:8 ESV

395. When you help the poor you are lending to the Lord—and he pays wonderful interest on your loan.

Proverbs 19:17 TLB

396. If you give, you will get! Your gift will return to you in full and overflowing measure, pressed down, shaken together to make room for more, and running over. Whatever measure you use to give—large or small—will be used to measure what is given back to you.

Luke 6:38 TLB

W. God wants us to live in peace and unity.

KEY VERSE

397. Become complete. Be of good comfort, be of one mind, live in peace; and the God of love and peace will be with you.

2 Corinthians 13:11 NKJV

398. By this all people will know that you are my disciples, if you have love for one another.

John 13:35 ESV

399. Behold, how good and pleasant it is for brethren to dwell together in unity.

Psalm 133:1 NKJV

400. Whoever loves his brother abides in the light, and in him there is no cause for stumbling.

1 John 2:10 ESV

401. Blessed are the peacemakers: for they shall be called the children of God.

Matthew 5:9 KJV

402. If we love our brothers and sisters who are believers, it proves that we have passed from death to life.

1 John 3:14 NLT

403. Joy fills hearts that are planning peace!

Proverbs 12:20 NLT

404. For though we have never yet seen God, when we love each other God lives in us and his love within us grows ever stronger.

1 John 4:12 TLB

405. If your enemies are hungry, give them food to eat. If they are thirsty, give them water to drink. You will heap burning coals of shame on their heads, and the LORD will reward you.

Proverbs 25:21–22 NLT

406. Dear children, let's not merely say that we love each other; let us show the truth by our actions. Our actions will show that we belong to the truth, so we will be confident when we stand before God.

1 John 3:18–19 NLT

407. Do not repay evil for evil or reviling for reviling, but on the contrary, bless, for to this you were called, that you may obtain a blessing.

1 Peter 3:9 ESV

408. Love your enemies! Do good to them. Lend to them without expecting to be repaid. Then your reward from heaven will be very great, and you will truly be acting as children of the Most High.

Luke 6:35 NLT

X. God calls us to witness for Him.

KEY VERSE

409. Follow Me, and I will make you fishers of men.

Matthew 4:19 NKJV

410. Godly men are growing a tree that bears life-giving fruit, and all who win souls are wise.

Proverbs 11:30 TLB

411. And those who are wise—the people of God—shall shine as brightly as the sun's brilliance, and those who turn many to righteousness will glitter like stars forever.

Daniel 12:3 TLB

412. Don't be afraid! Speak out! Don't quit! For I am with you and no one can harm you.

Acts 18:9–10 TLB

413. But you will receive power when the Holy Spirit has come upon you, and you will be my witnesses in Jerusalem and in all Judea and Samaria, and to the end of the earth.

Acts 1:8 ESV

414. The Holy Spirit will give you the right words even as you are standing there.

Luke 12:12 TLB

415. But the Helper, the Holy Spirit, whom the Father will send in my name, he will teach you all things and bring to your remembrance all that I have said to you.

John 14:26 ESV

416. I have put my words in your mouth and covered you in the shadow of my hand.

Isaiah 51:16 ESV

417. This will be your opportunity to bear witness.

Luke 21:13 ESV

418. For I will give you a mouth and wisdom, which none of your adversaries will be able to withstand or contradict.

Luke 21:15 ESV

419. Now go! I will be with you as you speak, and I will instruct you in what to say.

Exodus 4:12 NLT

420. The Sovereign LORD has given me his words of wisdom, so that I know how to comfort the weary.

Isaiah 50:4 NLT

421. Therefore thus says the LORD, the God of hosts: "Because you have spoken this word, behold, I am making my words in your mouth a fire."

Jeremiah 5:14 ESV

422. Let your light so shine before men, that they may see your good works and glorify your Father in heaven.

Matthew 5:16 NKJV

423. Let him know that whoever brings back a sinner from his wandering will save his soul from death and will cover a multitude of sins.

James 5:20 ESV

424. There will be glory and honor and peace from God for all who obey him, whether they are Jews or Gentiles.

Romans 2:10 TLB

425. Keep a close watch on yourself and on the teaching. Persist in this, for by so doing you will save both yourself and your hearers.

1 Timothy 4:16 ESV

426. For God is not unjust. He will not forget how hard you have worked for him and how you have shown your love to him by caring for other believers, as you still do.

Hebrews 6:10 NLT

427. Already the one who reaps is receiving wages and gathering fruit for eternal life, so that sower and reaper may rejoice together.

John 4:36 ESV

428. Therefore, my beloved brothers, be steadfast, immovable, always abounding in the work of the Lord, knowing that in the Lord your labor is not in vain.

1 Corinthians 15:58 ESV

429. So let's not get tired of doing what is good. At just the right time we will reap a harvest of blessing if we don't give up.

Galatians 6:9 NLT

*Whatever
is good and
perfect comes to
us from God, the
Creator of all light,
and he shines forever
without change
or shadow.*

James 1:17 TLB

God's Promises for Your Personal Needs

A. Do you have doubts and fears?

430. I can do all things through Christ who strengthens me.

Philippians 4:13 NKJV

431. Not that we are sufficient of ourselves to think of anything as being from ourselves, but our sufficiency is from God.

2 Corinthians 3:5 NKJV

432. He was fully convinced that God is able to do whatever he promises.

Romans 4:21 NLT

433. He who promised is faithful.

Hebrews 10:23 NKJV

434. Fear not, for I am with you. Do not be dismayed. I am your God. I will strengthen you; I will help you; I will uphold you with my victorious right hand.

Isaiah 41:10 TLB

435. I will not break my covenant; I will not take back one word of what I said.

Psalm 89:34 TLB

436. Indeed I have spoken it; I will also bring it to pass. I have purposed it; I will also do it.

Isaiah 46:11 NKJV

437. I am the Lord—I do not change.

Malachi 3:6 TLB

438. They will call on my name, and I will answer them. I will say, "These are my people," and they will say, "The LORD is our God."

Zechariah 13:9 NLT

439. Keep on asking, and you will receive what you ask for. Keep on seeking, and you will find. Keep on knocking, and the door will be opened to you. For everyone who asks, receives. Everyone who seeks, finds. And to everyone who knocks, the door will be opened.

Matthew 7:7–8 NLT

440. The prayer of a righteous person has great power as it is working.

James 5:16 ESV

441. He who calls you is faithful; he will surely do it.

1 Thessalonians 5:24 ESV

442. The sum of your word is truth, and every one of your righteous rules endures forever.

Psalm 119:160 ESV

443. They do not fear bad news; they confidently trust the LORD to care for them.

Psalm 112:7 NLT

444. The Lord is not slow to fulfill his promise as some count slowness, but is patient toward you, not wishing that any should perish, but that all should reach repentance.

2 Peter 3:9 ESV

445. He carries out and fulfills all of God's promises, no matter how many of them there are; and we have told everyone how faithful he is, giving glory to his name.

2 Corinthians 1:20 TLB

446. For the Lord God is our sun and our shield. He gives us grace and glory. The Lord will withhold no good thing from those who do what is right.

Psalm 84:11 NLT

447. You will make your prayer to him, and he will hear you.

Job 22:27 ESV

448. How true it is, and how I long that everyone should know it, that Christ Jesus came into the world to save sinners.

1 Timothy 1:15 TLB

449. Then you shall call, and the Lord will answer; you shall cry, and he will say, "Here I am."

Isaiah 58:9 ESV

450. The Lord hears his people when they call to him for help. He rescues them from all their troubles.

Psalm 34:17 NLT

451. Because of Christ and our faith in him, we can now come boldly and confidently into God's presence.

Ephesians 3:12 NLT

452. Know that the Lord has set apart for Himself him who is godly; The Lord will hear when I call to Him.

Psalm 4:3 NKJV

453. The eyes of the Lord are on the righteous, and His ears are open to their cry.

Psalm 34:15 NKJV

454. Do not seek what you are to eat and what you are to drink, nor be worried. . . . Instead, seek his kingdom, and these things will be added to you.

Luke 12:29, 31 ESV

B. Is it hard to keep your life clean?

455. Your sins are washed away, and you are set apart for God, and he has accepted you because of what the Lord Jesus Christ and the Spirit of our God have done for you.

1 Corinthians 6:11 TLB

456. Now all glory to God, who is able to keep you from falling away and will bring you with great joy into his glorious presence without a single fault.

Jude 24 NLT

457. If anyone is in Christ, he is a new creation; old things have passed away; behold, all things have become new.

2 Corinthians 5:17 NKJV

458. Already you are clean because of the word that I have spoken to you.

John 15:3 ESV

459. "Come now, let's settle this," says the LORD. "Though your sins are like scarlet, I will make them as white as snow. Though they are red like crimson, I will make them as white as wool."

Isaiah 1:18 NLT

460. He saved us, not because of the righteous things we had done, but because of his mercy. He washed away our sins, giving us a new birth and new life through the Holy Spirit. He generously poured out the Spirit upon us through Jesus Christ our Savior.

Titus 3:5–6 NLT

461. Though we are overwhelmed by our sins, you forgive them all.

Psalm 65:3 NLT

462. Christ also loved the church and gave Himself for her, that He might sanctify and cleanse her with the washing of water by the word.

Ephesians 5:25–26 NKJV

463. If we walk in the light, as he is in the light, we have fellowship with one another, and the blood of Jesus his Son cleanses us from all sin.

1 John 1:7 ESV

464. Just think how much more surely the blood of Christ will transform our lives and hearts. His sacrifice frees us from the worry of having to obey the old rules, and makes us want to serve the living God.

Hebrews 9:14 TLB

465. The LORD dealt with me according to my righteousness; according to the cleanness of my hands he rewarded me.

2 Samuel 22:21 ESV

466. A highway shall be there, and a road, and it shall be called the Highway of Holiness. The unclean shall not pass over it.

Isaiah 35:8 NKJV

467. Let us go right into the presence of God with sincere hearts fully trusting him. For our guilty consciences have been sprinkled with Christ's blood to make us clean, and our bodies have been washed with pure water.

Hebrews 10:22 NLT

468. Commit your work to the Lord, then it will succeed.

Proverbs 16:3 TLB

469. Let the wicked change their ways and banish the very thought of doing wrong. Let them turn to the LORD that he may have mercy on them. Yes, turn to our God, for he will forgive generously.

Isaiah 55:7 NLT

470. May your spirit and soul and body be kept strong and blameless until that day when our Lord Jesus Christ comes back again.

1 Thessalonians 5:23 TLB

471. Blessed are the pure in heart, for they shall see God.

Matthew 5:8 NKJV

C. Do you need peace of mind?

KEY VERSE

472. You will experience God's peace, which is far more wonderful than the human mind can understand. His peace will keep your thoughts and your hearts quiet and at rest as you trust in Christ Jesus.

Philippians 4:7 TLB

473. This righteousness will bring peace. Yes, it will bring quietness and confidence forever.

Isaiah 32:17 NLT

474. He speaks peace to his faithful people.

Psalm 85:8 NLT

475. Peace I leave with you; my peace I give to you. Not as the world gives do I give to you.

John 14:27 ESV

476. Come to me, all who labor and are heavy laden, and I will give you rest.

Matthew 11:28 ESV

477. The LORD will give strength to His people; The LORD will bless His people with peace.

Psalm 29:11 NKJV

478. For God gave us a spirit not of fear but of power and love and self-control.

2 Timothy 1:7 ESV

479. Those who love your instructions have great peace and do not stumble.

Psalm 119:165 NLT

480. He will keep in perfect peace all those who trust in him, whose thoughts turn often to the Lord.

Isaiah 26:3 TLB

481. Surely goodness and mercy shall follow me all the days of my life; And I will dwell in the house of the LORD forever.

Psalm 23:6 NKJV

482. You will have courage because you will have hope. You will take your time and rest in safety. You will lie down unafraid and many will look to you for help.

Job 11:18–19 TLB

483. He will shield you with his wings! They will shelter you. His faithful promises are your armor.

Psalm 91:4 TLB

484. No evil shall be allowed to befall you, no plague come near your tent.

Psalm 91:10 ESV

485. Don't be afraid, for I am with you.

Isaiah 43:5 TLB

486. If you lie down, you will not be afraid; when you lie down, your sleep will be sweet.

Proverbs 3:24 ESV

487. True godliness with contentment is itself great wealth.

1 Timothy 6:6 NLT

488. Your faith has saved you; go in peace.

Luke 7:50 TLB

489. Now may the Lord of peace himself give you peace at all times in every way.

2 Thessalonians 3:16 ESV

490. Don't love money; be satisfied with what you have. For God has said, "I will never fail you. I will never abandon you."

Hebrews 13:5 NLT

D. Are you often tempted?

491. In all these things we are more than conquerors through Him who loved us.

Romans 8:37 NKJV

492. God is faithful, and he will not let you be tempted beyond your ability, but with the temptation he will also provide the way of escape, that you may be able to endure it.

1 Corinthians 10:13 ESV

493. The Lord can rescue you and me from the temptations that surround us.

2 Peter 2:9 TLB

494. For because he himself has suffered when tempted, he is able to help those who are being tempted.

Hebrews 2:18 ESV

495. My grace is all you need. My power works best in weakness.

2 Corinthians 12:9 NLT

496. I have prayed for you that your faith may not fail.

Luke 22:32 ESV

497. I'm not asking you to take them out of the world, but to keep them safe from Satan's power.

John 17:15 TLB

498. Take heart, because I have overcome the world.

John 16:33 NLT

499. For everyone who has been born of God overcomes the world. And this is the victory that has overcome the world—our faith.

1 John 5:4 ESV

500. Resist the devil and he will flee from you.

James 4:7 NKJV

501. The God of peace will soon crush Satan under your feet.

Romans 16:20 TLB

502. For he will deliver you from the snare of the fowler and from the deadly pestilence.

Psalm 91:3 ESV

503. Do not be overcome by evil, but overcome evil with good.

Romans 12:21 NKJV

504. Let us hold fast the confession of our hope without wavering, for He who promised is faithful.

Hebrews 10:23 NKJV

505. Walk steadily forward to God without fear.

Job 11:15 TLB

506. Since future victory is sure, be strong and steady, always abounding in the Lord's work, for you know that nothing you do for the Lord is ever wasted.

1 Corinthians 15:58 TLB

507. Jesus gave his life for our sins, just as God our Father planned, in order to rescue us from this evil world in which we live.

Galatians 1:4 NLT

508. All who are victorious will inherit all these blessings, and I will be their God, and they will be my children.

Revelation 21:7 NLT

509. To him who overcomes I will grant to sit with Me on My throne, as I also overcame and sat down with My Father on His throne.

Revelation 3:21 NKJV

510. God blesses those who patiently endure testing and temptation. Afterward they will receive the crown of life that God has promised to those who love him.

James 1:12 NLT

511. Little children, you are from God and have overcome them, for he who is in you is greater than he who is in the world.

1 John 4:4 ESV

E. Are you hung up with guilt?

KEY VERSE

512. There is therefore now no condemnation for those who are in Christ Jesus.

Romans 8:1 ESV

513. Yet now God declares us "not guilty" of offending him if we trust in Jesus Christ, who in his kindness freely takes away our sins.

Romans 3:24 TLB

514. For God took the sinless Christ and poured into him our sins. Then, in exchange, he poured God's goodness into us.

2 Corinthians 5:21 TLB

515. And having chosen us, he called us to come to him; and when we came, he declared us "not guilty," filled us with Christ's goodness, gave us right standing with himself, and promised us his glory.

Romans 8:30 TLB

516. Everyone who trusts in him is freed from all guilt and declared righteous—something the Jewish law could never do.

Act 13:39 TLB

517. Having been justified by faith, we have peace with God through our Lord Jesus Christ.

Romans 5:1 NKJV

518. And because of what he has experienced, my righteous Servant shall make many to be counted righteous before God, for he shall bear all their sins.

Isaiah 53:11 TLB

519. Who dares accuse us whom God has chosen for his own? Will God? No! He is the one who has forgiven us and given us right standing with himself.

Romans 8:33 TLB

520. Who then will condemn us? Will Christ? No! For he is the one who died for us and came back to life again for us and is sitting at the place of highest honor next to God, pleading for us there in heaven.

Romans 8:34 TLB

521. Having now been justified by His blood, we shall be saved from wrath through Him.

Romans 5:9 NKJV

522. Christ's righteousness makes men right with God, so that they can live.

Romans 5:18 TLB

523. I, I am he who blots out your transgressions for my own sake, and I will not remember your sins.

Isaiah 43:25 ESV

524. As far as the east is from the west, so far does he remove our transgressions from us.

Psalm 103:12 ESV

525. I have swept away your sins like a cloud. I have scattered your offenses like the morning mist. Oh, return to me, for I have paid the price to set you free.

Isaiah 44:22 NLT

526. Their sins and iniquities will I remember no more.

Hebrews 10:17 KJV

527. He will again have compassion on us; he will tread our iniquities underfoot. You will cast all our sins into the depths of the sea.

Micah 7:19 ESV

528. I will forgive their iniquity, and their sin I will remember no more.

Jeremiah 31:34 NKJV

529. I will be merciful to their unrighteousness, and their sins and their iniquities will I remember no more.

Hebrews 8:12 KJV

530. He forgives all my sins. He heals me.

Psalm 103:3 TLB

531. So overflowing is his kindness toward us that he took away all our sins through the blood of his Son, by whom we are saved.

Ephesians 1:7 TLB

532. Though your sins are like scarlet, I will make them as white as snow. Though they are red like crimson, I will make them as white as wool.

Isaiah 1:18 NLT

533. I will cleanse away all their sins against me and pardon them.

Jeremiah 33:8 TLB

534. If anyone sins, we have an Advocate with the Father, Jesus Christ the righteous.

1 John 2:1 NKJV

535. He was pierced for our rebellion, crushed for our sins. He was beaten so we could be whole. He was whipped so we could be healed.

Isaiah 53:5 NLT

536. The blood of Jesus his Son cleanses us from every sin.

1 John 1:7 TLB

537. How much more shall the blood of Christ, who through the eternal Spirit offered Himself without spot to God, cleanse your conscience from dead works to serve the living God?

Hebrews 9:14 NKJV

538. Therefore I tell you, every sin and blasphemy will be forgiven people, but the blasphemy against the Spirit will not be forgiven. And whoever speaks a word against the Son of Man will be forgiven.

Matthew 12:31–32 ESV

539. Blessed is he whose transgression is forgiven, whose sin is covered.

Psalm 32:1 NKJV

540. What happiness for those whose guilt has been forgiven! What joys when sins are covered over! What relief for those who have confessed their sins and God has cleared their record.

Psalm 32:1–2 TLB

541. All we like sheep have gone astray; we have turned—every one—to his own way; and the LORD has laid on him the iniquity of us all.

Isaiah 53:6 ESV

542. If we confess our sins, He is faithful and just to forgive us our sins and to cleanse us from all unrighteousness.

1 John 1:9 NKJV

F. Does your life lack direction?

KEY VERSE

543. In everything you do, put God first, and he will direct you and crown your efforts with success.

Proverbs 3:6 TLB

544. The steps of good men are directed by the Lord. He delights in each step they take.

Psalm 37:23 TLB

545. I will lead them in paths they have not known. I will make darkness light before them, and crooked places straight. These things I will do for them, and not forsake them.

Isaiah 42:16 NKJV

546. I will instruct you and teach you in the way you should go; I will counsel you with my eye upon you.

Psalm 32:8 ESV

547. If you leave God's paths and go astray, you will hear a voice behind you say, "No, this is the way; walk here."

Isaiah 30:21 TLB

548. Commit your way to the LORD; trust in him, and he will act.

Psalm 37:5 ESV

549. The morning light from heaven is about to break upon us, to give light to those who sit in darkness and in the shadow of death, and to guide us to the path of peace.

Luke 1:78–79 NLT

550. The humble He guides in justice, and the humble He teaches His way.

Psalm 25:9 NKJV

551. For this great God is our God forever and ever. He will be our guide until we die.

Psalm 48:14 TLB

552. You will keep on guiding me all my life with your wisdom and counsel; and afterwards receive me into the glories of heaven!

Psalm 73:24 TLB

553. The LORD directs our steps, so why try to understand everything along the way?

Proverbs 20:24 NLT

554. If I take the wings of the morning and dwell in the uttermost parts of the sea, even there your hand shall lead me, and your right hand shall hold me.

Psalm 139:9–10 ESV

555. He leads me in paths of righteousness for his name's sake.

Psalm 23:3 ESV

556. For the Lord in his mercy will lead them beside the cool waters.

Isaiah 49:10 TLB

557. He makes me lie down in green pastures. He leads me beside still waters.

Psalm 23:2 ESV

558. When the Spirit of truth comes, he will guide you into all truth.

John 16:13 NLT

559. Thy word is a lamp unto my feet, and a light unto my path.

Psalm 119:105 KJV

560. I will direct their work in truth.

Isaiah 61:8 NKJV

561. A man's heart plans his way, but the LORD directs his steps.

Proverbs 16:9 NKJV

562. The LORD will guide you continually.

Isaiah 58:11 ESV

G. Are finances always a worry?

KEY VERSE

563. My God shall supply all your need according to His riches in glory by Christ Jesus.

Philippians 4:19 NKJV

564. Keep on asking, and you will receive what you ask for. Keep on seeking, and you will find. Keep on knocking, and the door will be opened to you.

Luke 11:9 NLT

565. Consider the ravens: they neither sow nor reap, they have neither storehouse nor barn, and yet God feeds them. Of how much more value are you than the birds!

Luke 12:24 ESV

566. Let him have all your worries and cares, for he is always thinking about you and watching everything that concerns you.

1 Peter 5:7 TLB

567. He gives us grace and glory. The LORD will withhold no good thing from those who do what is right.

Psalm 84:11 NLT

568. Your heavenly Father already knows all your needs.

Matthew 6:32 NLT

569. Until now you have asked nothing in my name. Ask, and you will receive, that your joy may be full.

John 16:24 ESV

570. Do not fear, little flock, for it is your Father's good pleasure to give you the kingdom.

Luke 12:32 NKJV

571. Trust in the LORD and do good. Then you will live safely in the land and prosper.

Psalm 37:3 NLT

572. I have been young and now I am old. And in all my years I have never seen the Lord forsake a man who loves him; nor have I seen the children of the godly go hungry.

Psalm 37:25 TLB

573. If you hard-hearted, sinful men know how to give good gifts to your children, won't your Father in heaven even more certainly give good gifts to those who ask him for them?

Matthew 7:11 TLB

574. Instead, seek his kingdom, and these things will be added to you.

Luke 12:31 ESV

575. It is better to have little and be godly than to own an evil man's wealth.

Psalm 37:16 TLB

576. Why, even the hairs of your head are all numbered. Fear not; you are of more value than many sparrows.

Luke 12:7 ESV

577. If God cares so wonderfully for flowers that are here today and thrown into the fire tomorrow, he will certainly care for you.

Luke 12:28 NLT

578. Your Father knows that you need these things.

Luke 12:30 NKJV

579. The LORD has remembered us; he will bless us.

Psalm 115:12 ESV

580. Therefore, obey the terms of this covenant so that you will prosper in everything you do.

Deuteronomy 29:9 TLB

581. They are like trees along a river bank bearing luscious fruit each season without fail. Their leaves shall never wither, and all they do shall prosper.

Psalm 1:3 TLB

582. Then you will prosper if you are careful to observe the statutes and the rules that the LORD commanded Moses for Israel. Be strong and courageous. Fear not; do not be dismayed.

1 Chronicles 22:13 ESV

583. As long as he sought the LORD, God made him prosper.

2 Chronicles 26:5 NKJV

584. Therefore I tell you, whatever you ask in prayer, believe that you have received it, and it will be yours.

Mark 11:24 ESV

585. Whatever you ask in my name, this I will do, that the Father may be glorified in the Son.

John 14:13 ESV

586. Yes, ask me for anything in my name, and I will do it!

John 14:14 NLT

H. Are you unhappy?

587. They that sow in tears shall reap in joy.

Psalm 126:5 NKJV

588. They weep as they go to plant their seed, but they sing as they return with the harvest.

Psalm 126:6 NLT

589. The joy of the LORD is your strength.

Nehemiah 8:10 NKJV

590. Our heart shall rejoice in Him, because we have trusted in His holy name.

Psalm 33:21 NKJV

591. I will rejoice in the LORD! I will be joyful in the God of my salvation.

Habakkuk 3:18 NKJV

592. I will see you again and then you will rejoice and no one can rob you of that joy.

John 16:22 TLB

593. The godly will rejoice in the LORD and find shelter in him. And those who do what is right will praise him.

Psalm 64:10 NLT

594. He heals the brokenhearted and binds up their wounds.

Psalm 147:3 NKJV

595. These things have I spoken unto you, that My joy might remain in you, and that your joy might be full.

John 15:11 NKJV

596. For the Kingdom of God is not a matter of what we eat or drink, but of living a life of goodness and peace and joy in the Holy Spirit.

Romans 14:17 NLT

597. You love what is good and hate what is wrong. Therefore God, your God, has given you more gladness than anyone else.

Psalm 45:7 TLB

598. With joy you will draw water from the wells of salvation.

Isaiah 12:3 ESV

599. You have let me experience the joys of life and the exquisite pleasures of your own eternal presence.

Psalm 16:11 TLB

600. Though you have not seen him, you love him. Though you do not now see him, you believe in him and rejoice with joy that is inexpressible and filled with glory, obtaining the outcome of your faith, the salvation of your souls.

1 Peter 1:8–9 ESV

601. But the righteous shall be glad; they shall exult before God; they shall be jubilant with joy!

Psalm 68:3 ESV

602. You will go out in joy, and be led forth in peace.

Isaiah 55:12 ESV

603. He has given me a new song to sing, of praises to our God. Now many will hear of the glorious things he did for me, and stand in awe before the Lord, and put their trust in him.

Psalm 40:3 TLB

604. But even if you should suffer for righteousness' sake, you will be blessed. Have no fear of them, nor be troubled.

1 Peter 3:14 ESV

605. Those who trust the LORD will be joyful.

Proverbs 16:20 NLT

606. In Your name they rejoice all day long, and in Your righteousness they are exalted.

Psalm 89:16 NKJV

607. You shall rejoice in all the good that the LORD your God has given to you and to your house.

Deuteronomy 26:11 ESV

608. Let all those rejoice who put their trust in You.

Psalm 5:11 NKJV

I. Do you need protection?

609. What's more, I am with you, and will protect you wherever you go.

Genesis 28:15 TLB

610. In peace I will lie down and sleep, for you alone, O LORD, will keep me safe.

Psalm 4:8 NLT

611. But all who listen to me shall live in peace and safety, unafraid.

Proverbs 1:33 TLB

612. The LORD is my light and my salvation; Whom shall I fear? The LORD is the strength of my life; Of whom shall I be afraid?

Psalm 27:1 NKJV

613. The beloved of the LORD shall dwell in safety by Him, who shelters him all the day long.

Deuteronomy 33:12 NKJV

614. For he orders his angels to protect you wherever you go.

Psalm 91:11 TLB

615. The Lord is a strong fortress. The godly run to him and are safe.

Proverbs 18:10 TLB

616. I will say of the LORD, "He is my refuge and my fortress; My God, in Him I will trust."

Psalm 91:2 NKJV

617. I am not ashamed, for I know whom I have believed and am persuaded that He is able to keep what I have committed to Him until that Day.

2 Timothy 1:12 NKJV

618. Though I walk in the midst of trouble, you preserve my life; you stretch out your hand against the wrath of my enemies, and your right hand delivers me.

Psalm 138:7 ESV

619. I will put you in the cleft of the rock and cover you with my hand until I have passed.

Exodus 33:22 TLB

620. He who dwells in the shelter of the Most High will abide in the shadow of the Almighty.

Psalm 91:1 ESV

621. Now who is there to harm you if you are zealous for what is good?

1 Peter 3:13 ESV

622. As the mountains surround Jerusalem, so the LORD surrounds his people, from this time forth and forevermore.

Psalm 125:2 ESV

623. The Angel of the Lord guards and rescues all who reverence him.

Psalm 34:7 TLB

624. When you go through deep waters, I will be with you. When you go through rivers of difficulty, you will not drown. When you walk through the fire of oppression, you will not be burned up; the flames will not consume you.

Isaiah 43:2 NLT

625. The good man does not escape all troubles—he has them too. But the Lord helps him in each and every one.

Psalm 34:19 TLB

626. For you are my hiding place; you protect me from trouble. You surround me with songs of victory.

Psalm 32:7 TLB

627. Now I know that the LORD saves his anointed; he will answer him from his holy heaven with the saving might of his right hand.

Psalm 20:6 ESV

628. He fills me with strength and protects me wherever I go.

Psalm 18:32 TLB

629. God is our refuge and strength, always ready to help in times of trouble.

Psalm 46:1 NLT

J. Is sickness a problem?

630. The prayer of faith will save the sick, and the Lord will raise him up.

James 5:15 NKJV

631. These miraculous signs will accompany those who believe: They will be able to place their hands on the sick, and they will be healed.

Mark 16:17–18 NLT

632. Admit your faults to one another and pray for each other so that you may be healed. The earnest prayer of a righteous man has great power and wonderful results.

James 5:16 TLB

633. He was pierced for our rebellion, crushed for our sins. He was beaten so we could be whole. He was whipped so we could be healed.

Isaiah 53:5 NLT

634. I will give you back your health again and heal your wounds.

Jeremiah 30:17 TLB

635. The LORD will take away from you all sickness, and none of the evil diseases of Egypt, which you knew, will he inflict on you.

Deuteronomy 7:15 ESV

636. The LORD sustains him on his sickbed; in his illness you restore him to full health.

Psalm 41:3 ESV

637. Each time he said, "No. But I am with you; that is all you need. My power shows up best in weak people." Now I am glad to boast about how weak I am; I am glad to be a living demonstration of Christ's power, instead of showing off my own power and abilities.

2 Corinthians 12:9 TLB

638. These troubles and sufferings of ours are, after all, quite small and won't last very long. Yet this short time of distress will result in God's richest blessing upon us forever and ever.

2 Corinthians 4:17 TLB

639. Then shall your light break forth like the dawn, and your healing shall spring up speedily; your righteousness shall go before you; the glory of the LORD shall be your rear guard.

Isaiah 58:8 ESV

640. Let all that I am praise the LORD; may I never forget the good things he does for me. He forgives all my sins and heals all my diseases.

Psalm 103:2–3 NLT

641. You shall serve the Lord your God only; then I will bless you with food and with water, and I will take away sickness from among you.

Exodus 23:25 TLB

642. Nevertheless the time will come when I will heal Jerusalem's damage and give her prosperity and peace.

Jeremiah 33:6 TLB

643. O my soul, don't be discouraged. Don't be upset. Expect God to act! For I know that I shall again have plenty of reason to praise him for all that he will do. He is my help! He is my God!

Psalm 42:11 TLB

644. I am the LORD, your healer.

Exodus 15:26 ESV

645. Anything is possible if you have faith.

Mark 9:23 TLB

646. He himself bore our sins in his body on the tree, that we might die to sin and live to righteousness. By his wounds you have been healed.

1 Peter 2:24 NLT

K. What about your friends?

KEY VERSE

647. Do not be deceived: "Bad company ruins good morals."

1 Corinthians 15:33 ESV

648. Therefore, if anyone is in Christ, he is a new creation; old things have passed away; behold, all things have become new.

2 Corinthians 5:17 NKJV

649. If we walk in the light, as He is in the light, we have fellowship one with another.

1 John 1:7 NKJV

650. There are "friends" who pretend to be friends, but there is a friend who sticks closer than a brother.

Proverbs 18:24 TLB

651. No longer do I call you servants, for the servant does not know what his master is doing; but I have called you friends, for all that I have heard from my Father I have made known to you.

John 15:15 ESV

652. Follow the steps of the godly instead, and stay on the right path.

Proverbs 2:20 TLB

653. Blessed is the man who walks not in the counsel of the wicked, nor stands in the way of sinners, nor sits in the seat of scoffers.

Psalm 1:1 ESV

654. A true friend is always loyal, and a brother is born to help in time of need.

Proverbs 17:17 TLB

655. Come out from among unbelievers, and separate yourselves from them, says the LORD. Don't touch their filthy things, and I will welcome you.

2 Corinthians 6:17 NLT

656. Be with wise men and become wise. Be with evil men and become evil.

Proverbs 13:20 TLB

657. You are my friends if you do what I command you.

John 15:14 ESV

L. Is a good reputation important?

658. Choose a good reputation over great riches; being held in high esteem is better than silver or gold.

Proverbs 22:1 NLT

659. A good reputation is more valuable than costly perfume.

Ecclesiastes 7:1 NLT

660. He will bring forth your righteousness as the light, and your justice as the noonday.

Psalm 37:6 ESV

661. Be happy if you are cursed and insulted for being a Christian, for when that happens the Spirit of God will come upon you with great glory.

1 Peter 4:14 TLB

662. It is an honor for a man to stay out of a fight. Only fools insist on quarreling.

Proverbs 20:3 TLB

663. You will be safe from slander; no need to fear the future.

Job 5:21 TLB

664. He will send down help from heaven to save me because of his love and his faithfulness.

Psalm 57:3 TLB

665. Listen to me, you who know right from wrong, you who cherish my law in your hearts. Do not be afraid of people's scorn, nor fear their insults.

Isaiah 51:7 NLT

666. Get rid of your sins and leave all iniquity behind you. Only then, without spots of sin to defile you, can you walk steadily forward to God without fear.

Job 11:14–15 TLB

667. He who is slow to anger is better than the mighty, and he who rules his spirit than he who takes a city.

Proverbs 16:32 ESV

668. In the cover of your presence you hide them from the plots of men; you store them in your shelter from the strife of tongues.

Psalm 31:20 ESV

M. Do you often feel insecure?

669. The eternal God is your dwelling place, and underneath are the everlasting arms.

Deuteronomy 33:27 ESV

670. God is our refuge and strength, a very present help in trouble.

Psalm 46:1 NKJV

671. Those who fear the LORD are secure; he will be a refuge for their children.

Proverbs 14:26 NLT

672. The LORD is their strength, and he is the saving refuge of His anointed.

Psalm 28:8 NKJV

673. I can do all things through him who strengthens me.

Philippians 4:13 ESV

674. The Lord is a strong fortress. The godly run to him and are safe.

Proverbs 18:10 TLB

675. To the poor, O Lord, you are a refuge from the storm, a shadow from the heat.

Isaiah 25:4 TLB

676. Though he fall, he shall not be cast headlong, for the LORD upholds his hand.

Psalm 37:24 ESV

677. Day by day the Lord observes the good deeds done by godly men, and gives them eternal rewards.

Psalm 37:18 TLB

678. The LORD is a shelter for the oppressed, a refuge in times of trouble.

Psalm 9:9 NLT

679. Those who know your name trust in you, for you, O LORD, do not abandon those who search for you.

Psalm 9:10 NLT

680. For the Lord says, "Because he loves me, I will rescue him; I will make him great because he trusts in my name."

Psalm 91:14 TLB

681. If God is for us, who can ever be against us?

Romans 8:31 NLT

682. The LORD is my helper; I will not fear. What can man do to me?

Hebrews 13:6 NKJV

683. For I, the LORD your God, hold your right hand; it is I who say to you, "Fear not, I am the one who helps you."

Isaiah 41:13 ESV

N. Do you need wisdom?

KEY VERSE

684. If any of you lacks wisdom, let him ask God, who gives generously to all without reproach, and it will be given him.

James 1:5 ESV

685. For God gives those who please him wisdom, knowledge, and joy.

Ecclesiastes 2:26 TLB

686. Blessed is the one who finds wisdom, and the one who gets understanding.

Proverbs 3:13 ESV

687. He will teach us His ways, and we shall walk in His paths.

Isaiah 2:3 NKJV

688. The wise of heart is called discerning.

Proverbs 16:21 ESV

689. I am the light of the world. If you follow me, you won't have to walk in darkness, because you will have the light that leads to life.

John 8:12 NLT

690. Evil people don't understand justice, but those who follow the LORD understand completely.

Proverbs 28:5 NLT

691. For the Lord grants wisdom! His every word is a treasure of knowledge and understanding. He grants good sense to the godly—his saints.

Proverbs 2:6–7 TLB

692. I will bless the Lord who counsels me.

Psalm 16:7 TLB

693. A wise man will hear and increase learning, and a man of understanding will attain wise counsel.

Proverbs 1:5 NKJV

694. We know that the Son of God has come, and he has given us understanding so that we can know the true God.

1 John 5:20 NLT

695. The fear of the LORD is the beginning of wisdom, and the knowledge of the Holy One is understanding.

Proverbs 9:10 NKJV

696. Whoever gets sense loves his own soul; he who keeps understanding will discover good.

Proverbs 19:8 ESV

697. The man who isn't a Christian can't understand and can't accept these thoughts from God, which the Holy Spirit teaches us. They sound foolish to him, because only those who have the Holy Spirit within them can understand what the Holy Spirit means. Others just can't take it in. But the spiritual man has insight into everything.

1 Corinthians 2:14–15 TLB

698. In all your ways acknowledge Him, and He shall direct your paths.

Proverbs 3:6 NKJV

699. Wisdom is a fountain of life to those possessing it.

Proverbs 16:22 TLB

700. True wisdom and power are God's. He alone knows what we should do; he understands.

Job 12:13 TLB

701. The mouth of the righteous brings forth wisdom.

Proverbs 10:31 ESV

702. We know about these things because God has sent his Spirit to tell us, and his Spirit searches out and shows us all of God's deepest secrets.

1 Corinthians 2:10 TLB

703. Whoever believes in him will not be put to shame.

1 Peter 2:6 ESV

O. Are you lonely?

KEY VERSE

704. I will never, never fail you nor forsake you.

Hebrews 13:5 TLB

705. For the mountains may depart and the hills disappear, but my kindness shall not leave you. My promise of peace for you will never be broken, says the Lord who has mercy upon you.

Isaiah 54:10 TLB

706. Truly our fellowship is with the Father and with His Son Jesus Christ.

1 John 1:3 NKJV

707. There are "friends" who pretend to be friends, but there is a friend who sticks closer than a brother.

Proverbs 18:24 TLB

708. Look! I have been standing at the door and I am constantly knocking. If anyone hears me calling him and opens the door, I will come in and fellowship with him and he with me.

Revelation 3:20 TLB

709. Draw near to God and He will draw near to you.

James 4:8 NKJV

710. I have set the LORD always before me; because He is at my right hand, I shall not be moved.

Psalm 16:8 NKJV

711. And he said, "My presence will go with you, and I will give you rest."

Exodus 33:14 ESV

712. I have loved you, O my people, with an everlasting love; with loving-kindness I have drawn you to me.

Jeremiah 31:3 TLB

713. The LORD will not reject his people; he will not abandon his special possession.

Psalm 94:14 NLT

714. I am the LORD; I have called you in righteousness; I will take you by the hand and keep you.

Isaiah 42:6 ESV

715. Yes, I will indeed do these things; I will not forsake them.

Isaiah 42:16 NLT

716. The Lord loves justice and fairness; he will never abandon his people. They will be kept safe forever.

Psalm 37:28 TLB

717. I have come that they may have life, and that they may have it more abundantly.

John 10:10 NKJV

718. Even if my father and mother abandon me, the LORD will hold me close.

Psalm 27:10 NLT

719. No, I will not abandon you or leave you as orphans in the storm—I will come to you.

John 14:18 TLB

P. Are you impatient for things to happen?

KEY VERSE

720. You need to keep on patiently doing God's will if you want him to do for you all that he has promised.

Hebrews 10:36 TLB

721. By your endurance you will gain your lives.

Luke 21:19 ESV

722. So let's not get tired of doing what is good. At just the right time we will reap a harvest of blessing if we don't give up.

Galatians 6:9 NLT

723. For everything there is a season, and a time for every matter under heaven.

Ecclesiastes 3:1 ESV

724. Rest in the Lord; wait patiently for him to act. Don't be envious of evil men who prosper. For the wicked shall be destroyed, but those who trust in the Lord shall be given every blessing.

Psalm 37:7–9 TLB

725. When the way is rough, your patience has a chance to grow.

James 1:3 TLB

726. When your patience is finally in full bloom, then you will be ready for anything, strong in character, full and complete.

James 1:4 TLB

727. May God, who gives this patience and encouragement, help you live in complete harmony with each other, as is fitting for followers of Christ Jesus.

Romans 15:5 NLT

728. Remain faithful even when facing death and I will give you the crown of life—an unending, glorious future.

Revelation 2:10 TLB

729. Finishing is better than starting. Patience is better than pride.

Ecclesiastes 7:8 NLT

730. Blessed is the man who remains steadfast under trial, for when he has stood the test he will receive the crown of life, which God has promised to those who love him.

James 1:12 ESV

731. All of you who endure to the end shall be saved.

Matthew 10:22 TLB

732. Behold, we consider those blessed who remained steadfast. You have heard of the steadfastness of Job, and you have seen the purpose of the Lord, how the Lord is compassionate and merciful.

James 5:11 ESV

733. I waited patiently for the LORD to help me, and he turned to me and heard my cry.

Psalm 40:1 NLT

734. Do not throw away your confidence, which has a great reward. . . . For yet a little while, and the coming one will come and will not delay.

Hebrews 10:35, 37 ESV

735. And it will be said in that day: "Behold, this is our God; We have waited for Him, and He will save us. This is the LORD; We have waited for Him; We will be glad and rejoice in His salvation."

Isaiah 25:9 NKJV

736. Believe that there is a God and that he rewards those who sincerely look for him.

Hebrews 11:6 TLB

737. We can rejoice, too, when we run into problems and trials for we know that they are good for us—they help us learn to be patient. And patience develops strength of character in us and helps us trust God more each time we use it until finally our hope and faith are strong and steady.

Romans 5:3–4 TLB

738. Wait patiently for the Lord. Be brave and courageous. Yes, wait patiently for the Lord.

Psalm 27:14 NLT

739. God has made an everlasting covenant with me; his agreement is eternal, final, sealed. He will constantly look after my safety and success.

2 Samuel 23:5 TLB

740. The prayer of a righteous person has great power as it is working.

James 5:16 ESV

741. But those who wait on the Lord shall renew their strength; They shall mount up with wings like eagles, they shall run and not be weary, they shall walk and not faint.

Isaiah 40:31 NKJV

Q. What if you are persecuted by others?

KEY VERSE

742. Blessed are those who are persecuted for righteousness' sake, for theirs is the kingdom of heaven.

Matthew 5:10 NKJV

743. If we endure, we shall also reign with Him.

2 Timothy 2:12 NKJV

744. If you cling to your life, you will lose it; but if you give it up for me, you will save it.

Matthew 10:39 TLB

745. Don't be bewildered or surprised when you go through the fiery trials ahead, for this is no strange, unusual thing that is going to happen to you. Instead, be really glad—because these trials will make you partners with Christ in his suffering, and afterwards you will have the wonderful joy of sharing his glory in that coming day when it will be displayed.

1 Peter 4:12–13 TLB

746. Be happy if you are cursed and insulted for being a Christian, for when that happens the Spirit of God will come upon you with great glory.

1 Peter 4:14 TLB

747. Do not say, "I will repay evil"; wait for the LORD, and he will deliver you.

Proverbs 20:22 ESV

748. Forgive, and you will be forgiven.

Luke 6:37 ESV

749. Blessed are the meek, for they shall inherit the earth.

Matthew 5:5 NKJV

750. I say, love your enemies! Pray for those who persecute you! In that way, you will be acting as true children of your Father in heaven.

Matthew 5:44–45 NLT

751. If your enemies are hungry, give them food to eat. If they are thirsty, give them water to drink. You will heap burning coals of shame on their heads, and the LORD will reward you.

Proverbs 25:21–22 NLT

752. The Lord your God fights for you, just as he has promised.

Joshua 23:10 TLB

753. You provide delicious food for me in the presence of my enemies. You have welcomed me as your guest; blessings overflow!

Psalm 23:5 TLB

754. Let all those rejoice who put their trust in You; Let them ever shout for joy, because You defend them.

Psalm 5:11 NKJV

755. The eternal God is your refuge, and his everlasting arms are under you. He drives out the enemy before you; he cries out, "Destroy them!"

Deuteronomy 33:27 NLT

756. He gives justice to all who are treated unfairly.

Psalm 103:6 TLB

757. For the LORD your God is he who goes with you to fight for you against your enemies, to give you the victory.

Deuteronomy 20:4 ESV

758. Though I walk in the midst of trouble, you preserve my life; you stretch out your hand against the wrath of my enemies, and your right hand delivers me.

Psalm 138:7 ESV

759. He will protect his faithful ones, but the wicked will disappear in darkness. No one will succeed by strength alone.

1 Samuel 2:9 NLT

760. The LORD your God is in your midst, a mighty one who will save; he will rejoice over you with gladness; he will quiet you by his love; he will exult over you with loud singing.

Zephaniah 3:17 ESV

761. The Lord will defeat your enemies before you; they will march out together against you but scatter before you in seven directions!

Deuteronomy 28:7 TLB

762. Behold, God will not reject a blameless man, nor take the hand of evildoers. He will yet fill your mouth with laughter, and your lips with shouting.

Job 8:20–21 ESV

763. The LORD opens the eyes of the blind. The LORD lifts up those who are bowed down.

Psalm 146:8 ESV

764. Give your burdens to the LORD, and he will take care of you. He will not permit the godly to slip and fall.

Psalm 55:22 NLT

765. For as we share abundantly in Christ's sufferings, so through Christ we share abundantly in comfort too.

2 Corinthians 1:5 ESV

766. We are pressed on every side by troubles, but we are not crushed. We are perplexed, but not driven to despair. We are hunted down, but never abandoned by God. We get knocked down, but we are not destroyed.

2 Corinthians 4:8–9 NLT

767. I have said these things to you, that in me you may have peace. In the world you will have tribulation. But take heart; I have overcome the world.

John 16:33 ESV

R. Are you grieving over something?

768. Even when walking through the dark valley of death I will not be afraid, for you are close beside me, guarding, guiding all the way.

Psalm 23:4 TLB

769. May our Lord Jesus Christ himself and God our Father, who has loved us and given us everlasting comfort and hope which we don't deserve, comfort your hearts with all comfort, and help you in every good thing you say and do.

2 Thessalonians 2:16–17 TLB

770. When the cares of my heart are many, your consolations cheer my soul.

Psalm 94:19 ESV

771. The Lord has comforted his people, and will have compassion upon them in their sorrow.

Isaiah 49:13 TLB

772. What a wonderful God we have—he is the Father of our Lord Jesus Christ, the source of every mercy, and the one who so wonderfully comforts and strengthens us in our hardships and trials. And why does he do this? So that when others are troubled, needing our sympathy and encouragement, we can pass on to them this same help and comfort God has given us.

2 Corinthians 1:3–4 TLB

773. I, I am he who comforts you.

Isaiah 51:12 ESV

774. The blessing of the LORD makes rich, and he adds no sorrow with it.

Proverbs 10:22 ESV

775. This is my comfort in my affliction, that your promise gives me life.

Psalm 119:50 ESV

776. Blessed are they who mourn, for they shall be comforted.

Matthew 5:4 NKJV

777. He knows the number of hairs on your head! Never fear, you are far more valuable to him than a whole flock of sparrows.

Luke 12:7 TLB

778. The Spirit of the Sovereign LORD is upon me, for the LORD has anointed me to bring good news to the poor. He has sent me to comfort the brokenhearted and to proclaim that captives will be released and prisoners will be freed. He has sent me to tell those who mourn that the time of the LORD's favor has come . . . To all who mourn in Israel, he will give a crown of beauty for ashes, a joyous blessing instead of mourning, festive praise instead of despair.

Isaiah 61:1–3 NLT

779. No, I will not abandon you or leave you as orphans in the storm—I will come to you.

John 14:18 ESV

780. Only then, without the spots of sin to defile you, can you walk steadily forward to God without fear. Only then can you forget your misery. It will all be in the past.

Job 11:15–16 TLB

781. The LORD is near to the brokenhearted and saves the crushed in spirit.

Psalm 34:18 NASB

782. Comfort, oh, comfort my people, says your God.

Isaiah 40:1 TLB

783. We know that all things work together for good to those who love God, to those who are the called according to His purpose.

Romans 8:28 NKJV

784. It is a broken spirit you want—remorse and penitence. A broken and a contrite heart, O God, you will not ignore.

Psalm 51:17 TLB

785. I will bless those who have humble and contrite hearts, who tremble at my word.

Isaiah 66:2 NLT

786. He heals the brokenhearted and binds up their wounds.

Psalm 147:3 NKJV

S. Do you often feel inadequate or frustrated?

KEY VERSE

787. The LORD is the source of all my righteousness and strength.

Isaiah 45:24 NLT

788. From his abundance we have all received one gracious blessing after another. For the law was given through Moses, but God's unfailing love and faithfulness came through Jesus Christ.

John 1:16–17 NLT

789. Because of him you are in Christ Jesus, who became to us wisdom from God, righteousness and sanctification and redemption.

1 Corinthians 1:30 ESV

790. For unto us a Child is born, unto us a Son is given; And the government will be upon His shoulder. And His name will be called Wonderful, Counselor, Mighty God, Everlasting Father, Prince of Peace.

Isaiah 9:6 NKJV

791. Because I live, you also will live.

John 14:19 ESV

792. I have been crucified with Christ. It is no longer I who live, but Christ who lives in me. And the life I now live in the flesh I live by faith in the Son of God, who loved me and gave himself for me.

Galatians 2:20 ESV

793. Commit your way to the LORD; trust in him, and he will act.

Psalm 37:5 ESV

794. Therefore he is able, once and forever, to save those who come to God through him. He lives forever to intercede with God on their behalf.

Hebrews 7:25 NLT

795. They are like trees along a river bank bearing luscious fruit each season without fail. Their leaves shall never wither, and all they do shall prosper.

Psalm 1:3 TLB

796. Whoever has the Son has life.

1 John 5:12 ESV

797. Overwhelming victory is ours through Christ who loved us enough to die for us.

Romans 8:37 TLB

798. Everyone can see how much he loves me. . . . His left hand is under my head and with his right hand he embraces me.

Song of Solomon 2:4, 6 TLB

799. Once you were dead because of your disobedience and your many sins. . . . For he raised us from the dead along with Christ and seated us with him in the heavenly realms because we are united with Christ Jesus.

Ephesians 2:1, 6 NLT

800. When you are being tempted, do not say, "God is tempting me." God is never tempted to do wrong, and he never tempts anyone else.

James 1:13 NLT

801. Let us therefore come boldly to the throne of grace, that we may obtain mercy and find grace to help in time of need.

Hebrews 4:16 NKJV

*Beloved, now
we are children
of God; and it has
not yet been revealed
what we shall be, but
we know that when He
is revealed, we shall be
like Him, for we shall
see Him as He is.*

1 John 3:2 NKJV

God's Promises
for Your Future Needs

A. What does the future hold? The return of Jesus Christ!

802. We look forward with hope to that wonderful day when the glory of our great God and Savior, Jesus Christ, will be revealed.

Titus 2:13 NLT

803. For the Lord himself will descend from heaven with a cry of command, with the voice of an archangel, and with the sound of the trumpet of God.

1 Thessalonians 4:16 ESV

804. They will see the Son of Man coming on the clouds of heaven with power and great glory.

Matthew 24:30 NKJV

805. Remember what I told you—I am going away, but I will come back to you again.

John 14:28 TLB

806. So be prepared, for you don't know what day your Lord is coming.

Matthew 24:42 TLB

807. For I know that my Redeemer lives, and at the last he will stand upon the earth.

Job 19:25 ESV

808. On that day his feet will stand on the Mount of Olives, east of Jerusalem.

Zechariah 14:4 NLT

809. Behold, he is coming with the clouds, and every eye will see him, even those who pierced him.

Revelation 1:7 ESV

810. May the Lord lead your hearts into a full understanding and expression of the love of God and the patient endurance that comes from Christ.

2 Thessalonians 3:5 NLT

811. When Christ who is your life appears, then you also will appear with him in glory.

Colossians 3:4 ESV

812. We know that when He is revealed, we shall be like Him, for we shall see Him as He is.

1 John 3:2 NKJV

813. You will see the Son of Man seated at the right hand of Power, and coming with the clouds of heaven.

Mark 14:62 ESV

814. So also Christ was offered once for all time as a sacrifice to take away the sins of many people. He will come again, not to deal with our sins, but to bring salvation to all who are eagerly waiting for him.

Hebrews 9:28 NLT

815. As you wait for the revealing of our Lord Jesus Christ, who will sustain you to the end, guiltless in the day of our Lord Jesus Christ.

1 Corinthians 1:7–8 ESV

816. So don't make judgments about anyone ahead of time—before the Lord returns. For he will bring our darkest secrets to light and will reveal our private motives.

1 Corinthians 4:5 NLT

817. They will look on me whom they have pierced and mourn for him as for an only son.

Zechariah 12:10 NLT

818. For as often as you eat this bread and drink the cup, you proclaim the Lord's death until he comes.

1 Corinthians 11:26 ESV

819. You also must be ready, for the Son of Man is coming at an hour you do not expect.

Luke 12:40 ESV

820. Most importantly, I want to remind you that in the last days scoffers will come, mocking the truth and following their own desires. They will say, "What happened to the promise that Jesus is coming again? From before the times of our ancestors, everything has remained the same since the world was first created." . . . But the day of the Lord will come as unexpectedly as a thief.

2 Peter 3:3–4, 10 NLT

821. Blessed are those servants whom the master, when he comes, will find watching.

Luke 12:37 NKJV

822. For as the lightning comes from the east and shines as far as the west, so will be the coming of the Son of Man.

Matthew 24:27 ESV

823. This Jesus, who was taken up from you into heaven, will come in the same way as you saw him go into heaven.

Acts 1:11 ESV

B. There will be a great resurrection of the dead in Christ.

824. For the trumpet will sound, and the dead will be raised incorruptible, and we shall be changed.

1 Corinthians 15:52 NKJV

825. The dead in Christ will rise first. Then we who are alive, who are left, will be caught up together with them in the clouds to meet the Lord in the air, and so we will always be with the Lord.

1 Thessalonians 4:16–17 ESV

826. An hour is coming when all who are in the tombs will hear his voice and come out.

John 5:28–29 ESV

827. Then, when our dying bodies have been transformed into bodies that will never die, this Scripture will be fulfilled: "Death is swallowed up in victory."

1 Corinthians 15:54 NLT

828. Thanks be to God, who gives us the victory through our Lord Jesus Christ.

1 Corinthians 15:57 ESV

829. This is the will of my Father, that everyone who looks on the Son and believes in him should have eternal life, and I will raise him up on the last day.

John 6:40 ESV

830. And if the Spirit of God, who raised up Jesus from the dead, lives in you, he will make your dying bodies live again after you die, by means of this same Holy Spirit living within you.

Romans 8:11 TLB

831. Just as each of us now has a body like Adam's, so we shall some day have a body like Christ's.

1 Corinthians 15:49 TLB

832. For since by man came death, by Man also came the resurrection of the dead. For as in Adam all die, even so in Christ all shall be made alive.

1 Corinthians 15:21–22 NKJV

833. I am the resurrection and the life. Whoever believes in me, though he die, yet shall he live.

John 11:25 ESV

834. This is the will of God, that I should not lose even one of all those he has given me, but that I should raise them to eternal life at the last day.

John 6:39 TLB

835. Our Savior Christ Jesus, who abolished death and brought life and immortality to light through the gospel.

2 Timothy 1:10 ESV

836. Since we believe that Jesus died and then came back to life again, we can also believe that when Jesus returns, God will bring back with him all the Christians who have died.

1 Thessalonians 4:14 TLB

837. He who raised the Lord Jesus will raise us also with Jesus and bring us with you into his presence.

2 Corinthians 4:14 ESV

C. You will receive heavenly rewards.

KEY VERSE

838. There is more than enough room in my Father's home. If this were not so, would I have told you that I am going to prepare a place for you? When everything is ready, I will come and get you, so that you will always be with me where I am.

John 14:2–3 NLT

839. According to his promise we are waiting for new heavens and a new earth, in which righteousness dwells.

2 Peter 3:13 ESV

840. Now the prize awaits me—the crown of righteousness, which the Lord, the righteous Judge, will give me on the day of his return. And the prize is not just for me but for all who eagerly look forward to his appearing.

2 Timothy 4:8 NLT

841. There will be no night there—no need for lamps or sun—for the Lord God will be their light; and they shall reign forever and ever.

Revelation 22:5 TLB

842. They desire a better country, that is, a heavenly one. Therefore God is not ashamed to be called their God, for he has prepared for them a city.

Hebrews 11:16 ESV

843. Thus we shall always be with the Lord.

1 Thessalonians 4:17 NKJV

844. They are before the throne of God, and serve Him day and night in His temple. And He who sits on the throne will dwell among them.

Revelation 7:15 NKJV

845. They shall hunger no more, neither thirst anymore; the sun shall not strike them, nor any scorching heat.

Revelation 7:16 ESV

846. For the Lamb in the midst of the throne will be their shepherd, and he will guide them to springs of living water, and God will wipe away every tear from their eyes.

Revelation 7:17 ESV

847. Remain faithful even when facing death and I will give you the crown of life—an unending, glorious future.

Revelation 2:10 TLB

848. Because I am righteous, I will see you. When I awake, I will see you face to face and be satisfied.

Psalm 17:15 NLT

849. Then the godly shall shine as the sun in their Father's kingdom.

Matthew 13:43 TLB

850. When Christ who is your life appears, then you also will appear with him in glory.

Colossians 3:4 ESV

851. The master was full of praise. "Well done, my good and faithful servant. You have been faithful in handling this small amount, so now I will give you many more responsibilities. Let's celebrate together!"

Matthew 25:21 NLT

852. Come, you who are blessed by my Father, inherit the kingdom prepared for you from the foundation of the world.

Matthew 25:34 ESV

853. Lay up for yourselves treasures in heaven, where neither moth nor rust destroys and where thieves do not break in and steal.

Matthew 6:20 ESV

854. Just as my Father has granted me a Kingdom, I now grant you the right to eat and drink at my table in my Kingdom. And you will sit on thrones, judging the twelve tribes of Israel.

Luke 22:29–30 KJV

855. Blessed be the God and Father of our Lord Jesus Christ! According to his great mercy, he has caused us to be born again to a living hope through the resurrection of Jesus Christ from the dead, to an inheritance that is imperishable, undefiled, and unfading, kept in heaven for you.

1 Peter 1:3–4 ESV

856. What we suffer now is nothing compared to the glory he will give us later.

Romans 8:18 TLB

857. For the Son of Man will come in the glory of His Father with His angels, and then He will reward each according to his works.

Matthew 16:27 NKJV

858. No eye has seen, nor ear heard, nor the heart of man imagined, what God has prepared for those who love him.

1 Corinthians 2:9 ESV

859. When the Chief Shepherd appears, you will receive the crown of glory that does not fade away.

1 Peter 5:4 NKJV

860. The one who conquers will have this heritage, and I will be his God and he will be my son.

Revelation 21:7 ESV

861. He will wipe away all tears from their eyes, and there shall be no more death, nor sorrow, nor crying, nor pain. All of that has gone forever.

Revelation 21:4 TLB

862. The one who conquers, I will grant him to sit with me on my throne, as I also conquered and sat down with my Father on his throne.

Revelation 3:21 ESV

863. After this I looked, and behold, a great multitude that no one could number, from every nation, from all tribes and peoples and languages, standing before the throne and before the Lamb, clothed in white robes, with palm branches in their hands.

Revelation 7:9 ESV

864. Well done, good and faithful servant; you have been faithful over a few things, I will make you ruler over many things. Enter into the joy of your lord.

Matthew 25:23 NKJV

865. Blessed are those who do His commandments, that they may have the right to the tree of life, and may enter through the gates into the city.

Revelation 22:14 NKJV

866. See, I am coming soon, and my reward is with me, to repay everyone according to the deeds he has done.

Revelation 22:12 TLB

867. He who testifies to these things says, "Surely I am coming quickly." Amen. Even so, come, Lord Jesus!

Revelation 22:20 NKJV

The Rev. David Wilkerson was perhaps best known for his early days of ministry to young drug addicts and gang members in New York City. His story is told in *The Cross and the Switchblade*, a book he co-authored in 1962 that has been read by more than fifteen million people in some thirty languages. The story was made into a Hollywood motion picture in 1970.

Rev. Wilkerson served as pastor in small churches in Pennsylvania until 1958, when he saw a photograph in *Life* magazine of several New York City teenagers charged with murder. Moved with compassion, he was drawn to the city and began a street ministry to what one writer called "desperate, bewildered, addicted, often violent youth." A year later, Rev. Wilkerson founded Teen Challenge in Brooklyn, which today reaches youth and adults with life-controlling problems through almost 1,200 centers in 91 countries.

Working under his global ministry, World Challenge, Inc., Rev. Wilkerson conducted evangelistic crusades and pastors' conferences, produced films, authored more than thirty books, including his recent *God Is Faithful*, and instituted feeding programs—which continue to this day—in some of the world's poorest areas.

In 1987, he founded Times Square Church in New York City. Today, the mission-focused congregation includes more than eight thousand people representing more than one hundred nationalities.

On April 27, 2011, Rev. Wilkerson posted this on his devotional blog: "To those going through the valley and shadow of death, hear this word: Weeping will last through some dark, awful nights, and in that darkness you will soon hear the Father whisper, 'I am with you. I cannot tell you why right now, but one day it will make sense. You will see it was all part of My plan. It was no accident.'" That afternoon, Rev. Wilkerson was killed in a car crash. His wife, Gwen, died on July 5, 2012. They are survived by their four children and their spouses, nine grandchildren, and five great-grandchildren.

To learn more about David Wilkerson's ongoing ministry, go to
http://www.worldchallenge.org.

To read more of David Wilkerson's daily devotions, go to
http://davidwilkersontoday.blogspot.com/.